REVELATION REVOLUTION
THE ANITCHRIST, ANGELS, & THE ABYSS

BY

DENNIS JAMES WOODS

LIFE TO LEGACY

Revelation Revolution
The Antichrist, Angels & the Abyss

by: Dennis James Woods, Copyright ©2020

ISBN-13: 978-1-947288-55-3

Printed in the United States
10 9 8 7 6 5 4 3 2 1

Cover design by: Legacy Design Inc
Legacydesigninc@gmail.com

Published by
Life To Legacy, LLC
P.O. 1239
Matteson, IL 60443
877-267-7477
www.Life2Legacy.com
Life2legacybooks@att.net

CONTENTS

It is completely astonishing that so many Christians put their hope in a rapture doctrine that at key points cannot be substantiated by the Scriptures. The average pretrib believer has no idea how the conclusions of that position were reached. All that they know is that the church will be gone before the trouble starts. The question is, what happens if their theory is wrong?

INTRODUCTION

In January 2018, *Newsweek* released an article titled, "Trump Will Start the End of the World, Claim Evangelicals Who Support Him."[1] The title of this article is indicative of a prevailing mindset that many Evangelicals, and other Protestants have concerning fundamental beliefs of how the world will end. The article begins by asking the question, why do so many Evangelicals support a man who clearly does not come close to living a life that reflects one who is a committed Christian. Trump made many campaign promises that were attractive to Evangelicals such as the appointment of conservative judges, overturning Roe vs. Wade, law and order, and border security. But the most important political agenda to Evangelicals was America's support of Israel. The question is, why is the support of Israel so important to Evangelicals?

On May 14th, 2018, at least two historic events took place in Jerusalem. The first was modern-day Israel's 70th national birthday and secondly, the United States moved its embassy from Tel Aviv to Jerusalem proclaiming Jerusalem as Israel's capitol. In attendance to this momentous occasion were several prominent Evangelical political and religious leaders from the United States and other nations. Many stated that the embassy move was historic and of great prophetic significance. In his address during the embassy ceremony, Israeli Prime Minister Benjamin Netanyahu gave a speech that made reference to Israel's historic temples. Netanyahu also recited the battle cry of the Israeli soldiers during the Six-Day War of 1967, "the temple mount is in our hands."

Throughout history, a temple has been central to Israel's identity. The first temple was Solomon's temple. The second Zerubbabel's temple, in which centuries later King Herod renovated and became known the Herodian temple. It was this same temple that Jesus referred to in His Mount Olivet Discourse concerning the signs of the end. Speaking of the Herodian temple Jesus stated "not one stone would be left upon an-

---

1 https://www.newsweek.com/trump-will-bring-about-end-worldevangelicals-end-times-779643

other." This prophecy was fulfilled in 70 A.D., when the Roman general Titus, destroyed that temple and the city of Jerusalem. Since 70 A.D., the Jews had been without a homeland and a temple. However, that all changed on May 14th, 1948 when Israel was re-established as a nation. For 70 years now, Israel has been back in their homeland. As some speculate, soon Israel will build a temple.

Central to end time prophetic fulfillment is the building of a third temple in Jerusalem. Prophecies such as Matthew 24:15, Daniel 9:27, and 2 Thessalonians 2:3, Rev. 11:1-2, and others, require a temple to be present in the "last days." It is this temple that the Antichrist will desecrate triggering what is known as "the Great Tribulation" the last three-and-one-half years of a seven-year period generally characterized as the "tribulation period." The tribulation period, occurs at the end of this current age, culminating with the battle of Armageddon, and the return of the Lord as King of Kings and Lord of Lords.

A fundamental eschatological position held by many Christians particularly those who are Evangelical is called the *pretribulational rapture position* or the pretrib rapture theory. In this theory, the temple will be built during the first half of the seven-year tribulation period. However, in the pretrib rapture theory, the rapture happens before the seven-year tribulation begins. Therefore, "anything" that gets Israel closer to that temple and seven-year period, signals a soon coming "rapture." This then was one of the most important linchpins between Donald Trump and Evangelicals, hence the title of the New York Times article, "Trump Will Start the End of the World." Therefore, to Evangelicals, Donald Trump is "God's man," and to use Trump's own self-aggrandizing words, he's "the chosen one." With key Evangelicals in his ear, Trump began fulfilling agenda items important to Evangelicals which comprise the majority of his base. On his own, Trump probably knew very little or could care less about end time Bible prophecy.

Along with his son-in-law Jared Kushner, in which the Kushner family are longtime friends of Netanyahu, Trump put forth an agenda to bring peace to the Middle East and cut "the deal of the century" in a peace treaty called the *Abraham Accords*. This got Evangelical prophecy juices flowing, especially when America moved its embassy to Jerusalem. The embassy move was perceived to be a huge step toward Israel building that long waited temple. The closer we get to the temple, the closer we get to the rapture. Therefore, even though Donald Trump was probably one of the most arrogant, immoral, lying, hate stoking, dog whistle blowing, race baiting, unconventional presidents America has had. Despite all of Trump's foul bombastic antics, Evangelicals nodded their heads while holding their noses. But since he was "God's man," who was going to bring about events that lead to the rapture, they kept silent and backed him.

But then comes the 2020 presidential election. Evangelical Christians were sure Trump would win. I received calls from Christian friends who were being lambasted by other Christians who chided "any believer who was not voting for Trump was not a Christian." "Trump is God's man," they insisted. They were positive and even prophesied that Trump would win—but that ain't what happened. Donald Trump was defeated. Evangelicals were stunned, in a state of disbelief, and some even bewildered. "How could God let this happen?" However, the problem wasn't with God, the problem was with what they believed. They assumed their agenda and God's agenda were one and the same, but clearly, they were not.

If the 2020 election results stumped Evangelicals, what would happen when they learn that the pretrib rapture theory itself, is wrong. You see, most Evangelicals have bought into the whole "Left Behind" scenario, where the world is thrown into chaos after the rapture happens, before the tribulation begins. Therefore, all of the things that Jesus, the apostle Paul, John and the Old Testament prophets, foretold, according to pretrib, has nothing to do with the Church, because born again believers will be raptured before that point.

So, what exactly is this pretrib doctrine based? Why would the average Christian place all their eggs in a pretrib basket? It is because they were all taught that the tribulation is a seven-year period where God would pour out His wrath on the earth. However, before that seven-year time period arrived, all born-again believers would be raptured away and thereby escaping the perils of this awful time. Will there be a rapture? Of course, the rapture is a biblical fact. However, the most important question is, Will there be a pretrib rapture?

Unfortunately, the average Christian who believes pretrib does not understand on what this doctrine is based. They only repeat what they have heard their pastors and teachers say, without studying it in any detail for themselves. They know all the talking points such as "God wouldn't beat up his bride before he marries her." Or, that the Holy Spirit and the Church has to be removed from the earth before the Antichrist can be revealed. "What comfort would there be if we were still here to be killed by the Antichrist?" "Certainly, Christ wouldn't let us go through that." However, just as they discovered after election 2020, no one has the market cornered on what God is about to do.

What many have not understood is that pretribulationism is a speculative doctrine and an unproven theory. The most appealing aspect of it is that it presents the path of least resistance. In this position, the Church is to be raptured before any of the events depicted in the Book of Revelation after chapter three, occurs. However, one of the consequences of being pretrib is that it can cause people to see end time prophecy as a secondary or even a tertiary subject and instill false hope. It can cause you to back an immoral man, as God's man, if he appears to be causing Bible prophecy to be fulfilled.

However, as ministers of the Gospel we should not encourage or promote the marginalization of Revelation which causes others not to study the only book of prophecy in the New Testament. From God's perspective, Revelation was so important, that there is a special blessing for those who read and keep those things that are written therein (Rev. 1:3). God loved the Church so much, that He sent John two-thousand years into the future, so we would know what would happen during the final days of this present age. But instead of heeding, we have marginalized its significance to the Church, and opted for a teaching that insist the prophecies of Revelation and other eschatological passages, have nothing to do with the Church—the very Church to whom it was written. However, instead of heeding this divinely inspired revelation, we have opted for a man-made doctrine that in many cases cannot be backed by the Scriptures. Pretrib is big on theological concepts, but often comes up very short on explicit biblical text to back up its many assertions.

So how and where did all of this start? And how have so many Christians bought into this teaching and what is this doctrine based upon? In the next chapter we cover the historical backdrop of how pretrib came to America.

1

The Impact of John Nelson Darby

During the 19th century, a trend developed in United States that promoted nondenominationism known as *The Bible Church Movement*. The chief proponent was an Anglican minister John Nelson Darby (1800-1882) who rejected the concept of a state church, while urging his followers to reject Christian denominations. Darby's view was controversial and radical for his time. His proposals included the separation from Christian denominations categorizing those organizations as apostate.[2]

In Darby's reasoning he thought of the true church as being temporary, and denominations as merely outward professions. This movement garnered the support of other influential ministers and associates of Darby such as revivalist Dwight L. Moody who also resisted denominationalism and led many inter-church crusades. Following in this trend, the historic Moody Memorial Church near downtown Chicago was one of the first nondenominational churches in the United States.[3]

After leaving the Church of England in 1831, Darby helped start a remarkably influential movement known as the *Plymouth Brethren*, a group that emphasized the study of ecclesiology and eschatology where he formulated much of his unique views on Bible prophecy. The Brethren fellowship was an "independent, nondenominational, evangelical movement who were dissatisfied with the formalism, clericalism and spiritual dryness of many British churches in the early 19th century. Christians of various groups met for Communion, prayer and Bible teaching based on a simplistic New Testament pattern, with centers in Dublin and Plymouth."[4] Darby emphasized the concept that organized Christianity was corrupt and therefore called for *ecclesiastical separation*. Spawning from his feeling

2 Dictionary of Christianity in America, pg 137, Bible Church Movement
3 Ibid, pg 137
4 Dictionary of Christianity in America pg 914, The Plymouth Brethren

of ecclesiological pessimism was Darby's distinctive position concerning the interpretation of prophetic events that involved a perspective on two separate and distinct programs for the Church and Israel. He promoted an interpretation of Scripture that taught a secret and pretribulational rapture of the Church. This new way of interpreting prophetic events of the Bible became known as *dispensationalism.*[5]

In Darby's view, God's plans were revealed through a series of covenants and coinciding dispensations, which were all foreshadows of the establishment of a Messianic kingdom on the earth. However, in the fullness of times when the Son of God came, His own people and nation Israel, rejected him. In response, God postponed the kingdom, turned away from Israel and created a new people for Himself consisting of Gentiles, called the Church.

According to Darby's dispensational view, God only resumes his works with the nation and people of Israel after he finishes building the Gentile Church, which abruptly ends at the rapture. Only then could the events depicted in Revelation chapters 4 through 19 such as the opening of the 7 seals, the blowing of the 7 trumpets, the revelation of the man of sin (the Antichrist), the consolidation of the ten-horn / ten-nation confederacy, the issuance of the mark of the beast, the 7 bowl judgments, Armageddon, Christ's second advent and the commencement of His thousand-year reign on earth called the Millennium, can occur. However, probably the most innovative yet disruptive aspect of Darby's teaching was his view of the secret and pretribulational rapture. This aspect of Darbyism was not received by everyone, most notably, members among the Plymouth Brethren, the group he established.[6]

After a significant clash between one of the Plymouth Brethren B. W. Newton and Darby over the "secret rapture," Darby propagated his views through prophetic conferences and Bible study groups.[7] In the 1870s, during a series of preaching tours, Darby's dispensationalism spread throughout America.[8] Darby's teachings influenced a number of evangelical pastors and teachers, including Dwight L. Moody, William E.

5 Dictionary of Christianity in America pg 339, John Nelson Darby
6 Ibid, pg 358, Dispensationalism
7 Ibid, pg 339, John Nelson Darby
8 Ibid pg 358, Dispensationalism

Blackstone, James H. Brookes, James M. Gray and probably the most influential of them all was Bible conference speaker, pastor and a former Confederate soldier of the 7th Regiment of Tennessee, C. I. Scofield.[9] Scofield was also influenced by James H. Brooks, one of the founders of the *Niagara Bible Conferences*, where dispensationalism was a favorite topic. Years after Darby's death, Scofield published his Dispensational views in a widely distributed and immensely popular Bible called the *Scofield Reference Bible.*

"In 1890, Scofield started a Bible Correspondence Course which he directed until 1914 when it was taken over by the Moody Bible Institute. Tens of thousands of students scattered over the world were indoctrinated with his dispensational ideas."[10] The Scofield Reference Bible was published in 1909 by Oxford University Press, expanded in 1917 and revised in 1967.[11] This Bible was the most important publication of the classic form of dispensationalism.[12] It was through the Scofield Reference Bible, that the *Pretrib rapture theory* became very popular and the preferred eschatological doctrine amongst fundamentalist and evangelicals. The Scofield Reference and Study Bible are still popular today, but not as much as it was when it was released in 1909. Other study bibles, such as the Ryrie Study Bible and many others, also promote dispensationalism.

Another major influencer was Lewis S. Chafer a Presbyterian minister and baritone soloist who sang for Dwight L. Moody during his famous conferences. In the fall of 1901, he met and became fascinated with C.I. Scofield after hearing him teach. Scofield became Chafer's mentor, and it was through that relationship with Scofield, that Chafer moved to New York and taught at Scofield's Bible Correspondence School.[13] As Chafer rose in prominence in the Bible conference movement, in 1924, he founded the Evangelical Theological College. In 1936, it was renamed Dallas Theological Seminary (DTS). DTS was soon recognized as one of the most prestigious seminaries teaching dispensational premillennialism and the pretrib rapture doctrine in the country.

---

9   Dictionary of Christianity In America, pg 1057, C.I. Scofield
10 The Story of Scofield's Life, Emma Moore Weston
11 Dictionary of Christianity In America, pg 1058, Scofield Reference Bible
12 The Encyclopedia of Christianity - Volume 1 (A-D), Dispensationalism pg 885
13 Dictionary of Christianity In America, pg 237, Lewis Sperry Chafer,

After Chafer's death in 1952, Dr. John Walvoord took over as Chancellor.[14] In 1997, it was Dr. Walvoord that I contacted to identify doctrinal problems of pretribulationism (more on this later). Influential alumni of DTS include: Hal Lindsey, Chuck Swindoll, Charles Ryrie, Dwight Pentecost, John Walvoord, J. Vernon McGee, Tony Evans, Zane Hodges, David Jeremiah, Andy Stanley, Robert Jeffress, Roy Zuck, Merrill Unger, Mark Hitchcock, Erwin Lutzer, Joesph Stowell, and many others.

Although some evidence for a pretrib rapture theory exists in the writings of the early Church Fathers and others throughout Church history, much of the dispensationalism and the pretrib rapture theory that we know today was systematized and popularized by Darby. Contributions to Darby's work came from other prominent scholars after him. In this author's opinion, the pretrib rapture doctrine itself cannot be exclusively laid at the feet of Darby; however, the growth of dispensationalism in America can be attributed to him.

To this day, the Pretribulation rapture doctrine is the prevailing eschatological view among Evangelicals, Fundamentalist, Pentecostals, Charismatics, and non-denomination Christians alike. This view is so passionately held, that in many circles if you teach anything other than pretrib, you can be disfellowshipped or declared a heretic.

In 1890, Darby published his own version of the New Testament, called the *Darby Translation*. His purpose in doing so was to make a translation for those who had no formal training in the original languages neither had   access to manuscript texts. "Darby's translation work was not intended to be read aloud. His work was for study and private use."[15] The Darby translation is rarely used by expositors, even those who are dispensational. Among the Darby translation critics were Charles Spurgeon.

---

14 Dictionary of Christianity In America, pg 237, Lewis Sperry Chafer, pg 237
15 https://www.biblegateway.com/versions/Darby-Translation-Bible/ (about the Darby translation)

2

SETTING THE STAGE

In the *Introduction*, a reference was made to a *Newsweek* article that said Evangelicals see Trump as ushering in the end of the world. When Trump moved the U.S. Embassy to Jerusalem as well as declared Jerusalem to be Israel's capitol, believers saw this as a major step toward Israel building their temple. Many believe that this temple will be built during Daniel's 70th week. However, when Trump lost the election many Evangelicals were stunned. They were forced to come to grips with the fact that they got it wrong about what they perceived to be Trump's role in fulfilling prophecy. However, an even greater problem is looming. Most Evangelicals are pretrib. They believe that the entire 7-year period, called the tribulation period is synonymous with the day of the Lord where God's wrath is poured out on the world. Since the Bible teaches that the Church is not appointed to wrath (1 Thes. 5:9), this requires the Church would be raptured before the 7-year period begins. According to pretrib theory, if Christians are still on earth during these events, that would mean they have entered the day of the Lord and have also missed the rapture.

During this Revelation Revolution series, we will test the validity of the 7-year day of the Lord time-frame along with addressing many other problems with pretribulationism. It is my belief that the church will not be prepared for the most turbulent time in human history. Millions of unsuspecting Christians are going to be caught flatfooted, when prophesied events occur. Since the 1800s, believers have been taught pretrib and promised that they were going to be raptured before the 70th week occurs. Are Christians setting up to be stunned once again? Have we seen this in history before?

THE THESSALONIAN DILEMMA

Before we delve into the mechanisms of pretribulationism, let's take a look at a church that was located in Macedon during the first century, a church to which Paul addressed two of his epistles. The place was Thessalonica and the epistles were addressed to the Thessalonians. During this time, there was persecution of Christians at the church of Thessalonica. Paul addressed this fact in second Thessalonians where he states;

> ...therefore, we ourselves speak proudly of you among
> the churches of God for your perseverance and faith in
> the midst of all your persecutions and afflictions which
> you endure. *This is* a plain indication of God's righteous
> judgment so that you will be considered worthy of the
> kingdom of God, for which indeed you are suffering.
>
> 2 Thessalonians 1:4-5

As it were with many Christian assemblies during the first centuries, persecution was a way of life. People were coming to Christ amidst pagan cult societies that typically worshiped various idols, gods, and goddesses. There was even a succession of Roman emperors that declared themselves to be God and whosoever would not bow down and worship them as God met gruesome public executions. Ironically, Christians were even martyred for being an atheist, because they refused to bow to the Roman Emperor as lord. Here is an excerpt from the account of the martyrdom of Polycarp, Bishop of the Church of Smyrna.

> On his confessing that he was, [the proconsul] sought
> to persuade him to deny [Christ], saying, "Have respect
> to thy old age," and other similar things, according to
> their custom, [such as], "Swear by the fortune of Cæsar;
> repent, and say, Away with the Atheists." But Polycarp,
> gazing with a stern countenance on all the multitude of
> the wicked heathen then in the stadium, and waving his
> hand towards them, while with groans he looked up to
> heaven, said, "Away with the Atheists." Then, the pro-
> consul urging him, and saying, "Swear, and I will set thee
> at liberty, reproach Christ;" Polycarp declared, "Eighty
> and six years have I served Him, and He never did me

any injury: how then can I blaspheme my King and my Saviour?"[16]

Like Polycarp, countless Christian believers died in the arenas while thousands of people cheered on as gladiators and wild animals tore believers to pieces. They developed all sorts of evil death contraptions to inflict as much suffering as possible, all while blood thirsty crowds were entertained. This author highly recommends incorporating the reading of *Foxx's Book of Martyrs* to Revelation studies as an adjunct to gain insight as it relates to Christianity under persecution.

Coming to grips with the persecution that historically accompanied Christians down through the centuries, will help take the sting out of the idea of the persecution of the saints found throughout the Revelation text. Because of the pretrib teaching, instead of embracing the legacy of persecution of Christians, and "the sufferings of Christ" somehow we have relegated that to history past and the "so-called" tribulation saints—that unfortunate group of "left behinds." As a result, particularly here in America, the idea of a persecuted Church is completely foreign and unfathomable.

As for the Thessalonians, their persecution was severe. But to make matters worse, apparently someone claimed to have apostolic authority, wrote a letter to the Thessalonians telling them that the persecution that they were undergoing was because they had entered the Day of the Lord. In response, this is what Paul wrote:

> Concerning the coming of our Lord Jesus Christ and our being gathered to him, we ask you, brothers and sisters, not to become easily unsettled or alarmed by the teaching allegedly from us—whether by a prophecy or by word of mouth or by letter—asserting that the day of the Lord has already come. Don't let anyone deceive you in any way, for that day will not come until the rebellion occurs and the man of lawlessness is revealed, the man doomed to destruction.
>
> 2 Thessalonians 2:1-3, NIV

---

16 Ante-Nicene Fathers – Vol. 1-Apostolic Fathers, Justin Martyr, Irena –Polycarp – the Martyrdom of Polycarp – Chapter 9 The Writings of the Fathers Down To A.D. 325

In my illustration at the beginning of the chapter, Christians were panicking because they were taught that the signing of the seven-year covenant that starts Daniel's 70th Week, the seven-year period that pretrib teaches coincides with the Day of the Lord. The illustration that I laid out is conceptually similar to the circumstances that occurred to the saints at Thessalonica. As the passage implies someone had written a false letter claiming to be from Paul saying that the day of the Lord was already upon them. This caused serious problems for them, leaving them "shaken in mind and troubled," (confused and gripped in fear). Paul had already taught them that they wouldn't go through the day of the Lord (the wrath of God), but now because of the bogus letter which they accepted to be authentic, they found themselves in the midst of what they mistakenly believed to be the day of the Lord.

Just as the Thessalonians of old received the bogus letter as an official doctrinal position, modern day Christians that adhere to pretrib would also be in a similar circumstance causing them to be "shaken in mind" as they are confronted with being in that 7-year tribulation period that pretrib promised they would escape. They too, would have their faith shaken, just as the Thessalonians of antiquity did. If they thought they were in Daniel's 70th week, that 7-year tribulation period, which they accept as the day of the Lord, certainly, it would mean that they have missed the rapture. Therefore, finding themselves in the 70th week of Daniel, what hope would they have if they believe they've missed their blessed hope?

Erroneous resurrection doctrines were not uncommon during Paul's days. The Bible records, there was another doctrine that was destroying people's faith. Paul had to write in 2 Timothy about the doctrine of *Hymenreus and Philetus,* that taught that the resurrection had occurred already, which overthrew the faith of the people (2 Tim. 2:18). He had to address a similar doctrine in 1 Corinthians 15:12, which said there was no resurrection. Clearly, Paul tells us that without the hope of the resurrection, preaching, our faith, and this life, is all in vain. The thought of missing the resurrection would be devastating to any generation of Christians, just as it was in Paul's day.

What a reality check. Being in the midst of Daniel's 70th week and now realizing that they had been taught the wrong thing or had missed the rapture, would result in overwhelming fear in the face of severe persecution. With the real possibility of death, modern Christians would be faced with the historic reality that many generations of Christians lived with daily. Many Christians will defect left and right, just as the Bible says; *there will be a falling away first.* How many of those unsuspecting Christians who thought they would be raptured away would stand if their freedom was threatened? How many would remain faithful if their finances and resources were cut off? How many would hold on to Christ if their family members were incarcerated or even worse, were executed?

These are realities that past Christians in the body of Christ lived with every day of their lives. Although the Bible clearly teaches that "the Beast shall make war with the saints and overcome them" (Dan. 7:21, Rev.13:6), pretrib does some theological gymnastics and has created a whole other group of Christians, who they claim are not a part of the Church but are some second-class group of believers that were summarily "left behind." But is this the case? In the coming chapters of this book we will be examining some major flaws of pretribulationism. I guarantee, you will never see pretrib or the book of Revelation the same way again.

3
FILLING IN THE BLANKS

Before we grapple with the key fallacies of pretribulationism as it relates to Second Thessalonians, I would like to pose two questions.
Why is the book of Revelation necessary? The simple answer is, the
Lord wanted us to know what was coming. The second question is, why
did He want us to know what's coming? One way of answering this
complex question is by referring to what Jesus and the prophets of old
have stated about the period in which Revelation addresses. The times
in which Revelation speaks of are unique because there has never been
a period in the history of the world like those prophesied in Revelation.
Jesus warned, "For those days will be a time of tribulation *such as has not
occurred since the beginning of the creation which God created until now, and never
will"* (Mark 13:19).

Joel also weighs in when he writes, "For the day of the LORD is coming;
"Surely it is near, A day of darkness and gloom, A day of clouds and
thick darkness. As the dawn is spread over the mountains...There has
never been *anything* like it, Nor will there be again after it to the years
of many generations"(Joel 2:1-2). The Prophet Daniel also echoes the
uniqueness of the times when he prophesies: "...And there will be a
time of distress such as never occurred since there was a nation until
that time..." (Daniel 12:1).

From Old and New Testament perspectives, the Day of the Lord has no
historic reference point in which to look back to. It has no equal to compare.
There are no times or epochs like it. If you took all the calamitous events
of the world and throughout human history, you wouldn't find anything
that could equate with the magnitude and greatness of this period. There
will be disturbances both in heaven and on earth. In Luke, Jesus declares,

> And there shall be signs in the sun, and in the moon, and in the
> stars; and upon the earth distress of nations, with perplexity; the

sea and the waves roaring; Men's hearts failing them for fear, and for looking after those things which are coming on the earth: for the powers of heaven shall be shaken. Luke 21:25-26, KJV

It is because of the uniqueness of that time, with no parallel to contrast it to, that I believe God gave us the book of Revelation. The book of Revelation fills in the blanks on a time coming that has no equal. Revelation compensates for the unique severity of the time, by counterbalancing it with God's revealed foreknowledge. In God's divine love and concern for the redeemed whether Jew or Gentile, that He in a great act of love, transported a human being thousands of years in the future, to write down events that were in some cases, beyond the apostle's ability to comprehend. God accommodates us. He condescends to our frailty and in a divine act of compassion gives us a play-by-play prophetic peek into a future event that has no historic or human frame of reference. Therefore, it was necessary for Revelation to be added to the canon of Scripture, because after the canon was closed there would be no chance of adding it later. Therefore, God gave us the end from the beginning, which is always God's fingerprint.

Revelation is not simply some prophetic information for scholars to debate. God saw the need to inform us on things to come, so that we will be able to endure during a time that will try men's souls. Of these things Jesus emphasized, "Behold, I have told you in advance" (Matthew 24:25). Advanced warning is the greatest weapon to fight against the uncertainty and the vicissitudes of tumultuous times. How many times have we all said, "if I only knew ahead of time, I would have did things differently."

Jesus' forewarning and foreknowledge is a divine prerogative of His sovereignty, which in many cases is hidden from humankind. But not in this case, He is telling us ahead of time so the generation that will face the apocalyptic Antichrist, will respond with the same fortitude as the saints of old, when they faced their historic antichrists. In this way, the saints of the fledgling church, and saints of the eschatological church will have the same thing in common, faith under fire during a period of upheaval and severe persecution.

The worse thing that antichrists of the past, or the one that will come can do, is kill the body. That's it. He has no power beyond that. This is why Jesus warned "I tell you, my friends, do not be afraid of those who kill the body and after that can do no more. But I will show you whom you should fear: Fear him who, after your body has been killed, has authority to throw you into hell. Yes, I tell you, fear him" (Luke 12:4-5, NIV). No matter what comes in the future, stand in the assurance that the apostle Paul gives us when he declares:

> Who will separate us from the love of Christ? Will tribulation, or distress, or persecution, or famine, or nakedness, or peril, or sword? Just as it is written, "FOR YOUR SAKE WE ARE BEING PUT TO DEATH ALL DAY LONG; WE WERE CONSIDERED AS SHEEP TO BE SLAUGHTERED." But in all these things we overwhelmingly conquer through Him who loved us. For I am convinced that neither death, nor life, nor angels, nor principalities, nor things present, nor things to come, nor powers, nor height, nor depth, nor any other created thing, will be able to separate us from the love of God, which is in Christ Jesus our Lord.
>
> Romans 8:35-39

This is a powerful passage. Paul has covered the gamut of possibilities in all creation, in the visible or invisible realms, that can come against God's people. The conclusion is there is nothing in all creation whether of human or supernatural agency, geographical, cosmological, angelic, demonic, whether past, present, or future, absolutely nothing—including the Antichrist, Satan, or the False Prophet can be able to separate us from the love of God that's in Christ Jesus. Here in this passage, Paul marginalizes death's sting when he says, "for your sake we are killed all day long being sheep for the slaughter." It is if though the apostle was saying martyrdom is a believer's glorious legacy. It is quite fitting that we too should lay down our lives for the One that laid down His life for us. Before he was beheaded, Paul wrote these words to Timothy,

> For I am now ready to be offered, and the time of my departure is at hand. I have fought a good fight, I have finished *my* course, I have kept the faith: Henceforth there is laid up for me a crown of righteousness, which the Lord, the righteous judge, shall give me at that day: and not to

> me only, but unto all them also that love his appearing. 2
> Timothy 4:6

Paul's language here is not incidental. Obviously, by this time he knows that he was about to be executed, and he realized the rapture wasn't going to happen before he was beheaded. However, Paul was resolute and unmovable. His characterization of his circumstance is interesting. Paul does not consider himself to be a victim of unfortunate circumstances, but likens himself to be a *drink offering* (NIV) ready to be poured out. Truly, Paul was a living sacrifice, holy, acceptable and pleasing to God.

Paul was able to have the outlook that he had because he was comforted in his tribulation. This is the ministry of the Holy Spirit who gives peace and comfort in the face of impending death. We see this same comforting phenomenon with Stephen, who was "full of the Spirit," when he was about to die the barbaric death of stoning. Incredibly, he was more concerned about his killers than himself. "He kneeled down, and cried with a loud voice, Lord, lay not this sin to their charge" (Acts 7:55,60,KJV).

This is only possible through the indwelling of the Comforter. Ironically, pretribulationists often use 1 Thessalonians 4:18 "Wherefore, comfort one another with these words" as a basis to teach comfort in the sense of the cessation or the avoidance of suffering or tribulation. Citing 1 Thes. 4:18, they assert, "what comfort would it be, if the church was still here to be martyred by Antichrist? Who could experience comfort in that?" However, this is a shortsighted point of view because the Thessalonians were indeed experiencing severe persecution. Not experiencing or avoiding persecution was not the point.

The comfort in which Paul spoke was not based upon escaping persecution or death. The Thessalonians were persecuted. Paul he was beheaded. However, it's knowing that God had counted them worthy to suffer on His behalf. They were also assured that their dead loved ones would still partake in Christ's glorious return for the church. If Paul was teaching an imminent pretrib rapture, he would have said, be comforted in the fact that the Lord could come at any minute now to deliver you from tribulation and end your suffering. But Paul didn't tell them that because he couldn't say that. Why? Because the Lord (not Paul) knew that two-thousand years and running, the rapture wasn't going to happen.

Therefore, if Paul or anyone else believed that the Lord was coming any time prior to the 21st century, they were wrong, and we have two-thousand years of waiting to prove that. When we are told to "look for" or to "wait for" the Lord, the Lord is speaking collectively to all Christians of all ages. The Bible also speaks in terms of "we shall be caught up" because it applies to all generations of church saints from the Day of Pentecost to the rapture. "We" is indicative of inclusion, not a specific generation. It applies to all true Christians, no matter when the rapture occurs. I am not suggesting that first century Christians didn't expect Christ to come in their life time. But, I am saying if they did expect it then obviously they were wrong.

Through God's love and concern for the Church, He wrote Revelation so the Church would be prepared for the turbulent times that would precede God pouring out His wrath on the world. However, instead of the Church being prepared, modern day Christians particularly in the West and America, have mainly ignored the message of Revelation because the most popular eschatological doctrine "The Pretribulation Rapture Theory" insists that the Church will not experience any of the events found in Revelation between chapters 4 and 19. Therefore, the purpose of Revelation has been undermined by doctrines of men, a theological, ideological position that is most popular with the majority of Christians because we avoid all the trouble. However, historically, that has never been the case. Christians have always endured tribulation and paid for their faith with their lives, which still occurs to this day.

Make no mistake about it, pretrib is an expansive doctrine, and a well structured theological position written by some very smart people. Probably the most attractive aspect of pretrib is, it answers so many tough questions. That's what people want is answers to their questions. Provide the answers, and tell them not to worry about what occurs in Revelation because the Church won't be here, that's enough for the vast majority of Christians, who frankly do not want to deal with the idea of suffering anyway. Getting through today and taking care of their daily affairs and families are enough. Yes indeed, provide the answers, but also tell them the whole truth. Don't just teach Revelation and rapture doctrines as if pre-trib is the only way things can turn out. Teach the flip side of the coin as well.

When has any doctrine or plan that people have constructed, aligned perfectly with how God actually manifests His prophetic plan in time and space? Though there were numerous prophecies that foretold the coming of Christ, people still missed it when He came, particularly the scholars of that day. The Pharisees who were the scholars, the professors, and the educators turned out to be Christ's most ardent opposers. He didn't fit into their theological schemes. Jesus was an existential threat to their doctrines and traditions. People love the doctrines and traditions that they create more than they do God's Word. This has always been the case, and it still the same way today.

Since pretrib is so widely and passionately held, it's not just a doctrine, but it has become a tradition. Most people that believe pretrib believe it traditionally, not doctrinally, because the average person does not know the specifics of the doctrine. What they really know is, "the Church is not going to be here." Once doctrine becomes tradition, people become very guarded and protective concerning their traditional beliefs. A colleague once told me about trying to show an associate where pretrib was wrong. Ironically, the person didn't know what Scriptures to quote to defend pretrib, but cited what occurred in the movie *Left Behind*. Unfortunately, pretrib proponents are guaranteeing that Christians will be caught up in a pretrib rapture based on a speculative doctrine, and have not been honest with the people by telling them that their position like all the rest, are theories and not proven facts. They are making promises on things of God in which they have no control. That's a problem because pretrib provides the proverbial security blanket that allows Christians not to think about what's coming.

There are two ways this can end up. If pretrib theory is correct, then all the Christians are gone before Daniel's 70th week occurs. If that's the case, then Hallelujah! However, if pretrib theory is incorrect, then what will happen? Millions of Christians around the world will still be here to experience the events in Revelation, that they were assured they would miss. Under these circumstances, there will be confusion, hysteria, and compromise which will lead to a mass falling away from the faith. I bring this scenario up because there are serious flaws in the pretrib theory. This book is the first edition of several forthcoming editions that will expose the fallacies of pretrib. What follows is just the beginning.

4

Is the Holy Spirit the Restrainer of

2 Thessalonians 2

Recently, I was listening to one of the top Evangelical pastors in the country teach on end-time prophecy and the rapture of the Church. He spoke of how terrible the world will be during those times, but emphasized how much worse it will be when the Holy Spirit is removed from the earth. The pastor went on to quote 2 Thessalonians 2:6-9 as a proof text for this concept of the removal of the Holy Spirit as the restrainer from the earth, at which time *the Church* which is the corporate temple of the Holy Spirit will simultaneously be translated.

Others have characterized this event as "the reversal of Pentecost,"[17] meaning that just as the Holy Spirit came in Acts 2:1-21, it will be removed in similar fashion before the Antichrist is revealed. Though some scholars refer to this event as a so-called *reversal of Pentecost*, there are no Scriptures anywhere in the Bible that backs the idea that Pentecost will be reversed. That is a theological conclusion based on an interpretive speculation of the 2 Thes. 2:6-7 text, that the "he" is the Holy Spirit.

Clearly the outpouring of the Spirit is well documented in the Scriptures in both Old and New Testaments (Joel 2:28-32, Acts 2:1-21). We have explicit text unambiguously showing the coming, or the outpouring of the Spirit, but there are *no texts* anywhere in Scripture showing the reversal of Pentecost in a similar manner which it came.

In this chapter, we will be unraveling the mystery of the restrainer. The controversy begins with the following text.

> 3) Don't let anyone deceive you in any way, for that day
> will not come until the rebellion occurs and the man of

---

17 Things To Come, J. Dwight Pentecost, Chap. 17, pg 262

lawlessness is revealed, the man doomed to destruction.

4) He will oppose and will exalt himself over everything that is called God or is worshiped, so that he sets himself up in God's temple, proclaiming himself to be God.

5) Don't you remember that when I was with you I used to tell you these things?

6) And now you know what is holding him back, so that he may be revealed at the proper time. 7) For the secret power of lawlessness is already at work; but the one who now holds it back will continue to do so till he is taken out of the way.

8) And then the lawless one will be revealed, whom the Lord Jesus will overthrow with the breath of his mouth and destroy by the splendor of his coming.
2 Thessalonians 2:3-8, NIV

Speaking of the first twelve verses of 2 Thessalonians 2, John Walvoord observes, "This section of verses contains information found nowhere else in the Bible. It is key to understanding future events and is central to this epistle."[18] Walvoord could not have been more correct. The above passage is essential in order to be able to unpack all the eschatological truths laden in this text, but it is also where pretribulationism has steered most of Christianity in the wrong direction. According to verse 3, "that day" (meaning the Day of the Lord) will not come until two identifiable events occur. The first being "until the rebellion occurs" and the second "the man of lawlessness is revealed."

THE REBELLION
The word *rebellion*, comes from the Greek word *apostasia*[19] which means *defiance of established system or authority, rebellion, abandonment, breach of faith, of the rebellion caused by the Lawless One in the last days.* In the King James Version, *apostasia* is translated *falling away.* What exactly is this *falling away* is not certain, but some interpret it to be a mass falling away during the time of the Antichrist as suggested in the definition above (BDAG).

18 The Bible Knowledge Commentary, New Testament, 2 Thessalonians chapter 2, pg 717
19 BDAG, A Greek-English Lexicon of the New Testament and Other Early Christian Literature, *apostasia*
-25-

Others support a gradual slipping away of professing Christians through compromise with the world. In any event, Paul seems to have a specific event in mind, because this will be a direct sign that the day of the Lord is very near. We will pick up the discussion on what could be the possible cause of this rebellion later.

THE MAN OF SIN REVEALED

The second event Paul describes that must occur prior to the day of the Lord is found in verse 3 is, "the man of lawlessness is revealed, the man doomed to destruction." The KJV says it this way "...and that man of sin be revealed, the son of perdition; 2 Thessalonians 2:3. How and when the Antichrist will be revealed will be taken up in great detail later. The next important aspect to be emphasized comes in verses 6 and 7 where Paul discusses *something* or *someone* holding back the revealing of the Antichrist. This is where all the controversy lies. The text reads:

> KJV
>
> Remember ye not, that, when I was yet with you, I told you these things? And now ye know what withholdeth that he might be revealed in his time. For the mystery of iniquity doth already work: only he who now letteth *will let*, until he be taken out of the way. 2 Thessalonians 2:5-7
>
> NASB
>
> And you know what restrains him now, so that in his time he will be revealed. For the mystery of lawlessness is already at work; only he who now restrains *will do so* until he is taken out of the way. 2 Thessalonians 2:6-7

Admittedly, this is one of the most difficult passages in 2 Thessalonians. F.F. Bruce observes "and, as it is, you know what is restraining him. They knew because they had been told; later readers are at a disadvantage compared with them and have to guess."[20] I agree with Dr. Bruce's statement because it is in "the guessing" that has caused a great amount of doctrinal speculation. For within pretribulationism, a great deal rest on

---

20 Word Biblical Commentary, Vol. 45 F.F. Bruce, 1 & 2 Thessalonians, pg 169

how one fills in the blanks on whom the restrainer of 2 Thessalonians 2 is. Throughout the centuries past, a number of suggestions have been forwarded as to answer the compelling question, who is "the restrainer?" The following are just a few options as listed in *The Believer's Commentary*.[21] 1) The Roman Empire, 2) The Jewish State, 3) Satan, 4) The principle of law and order found in human government, 5) God, 6) The Holy Spirit, 7) The Holy Spirit and the Church. Dwight Pentecost gives a similar list in his celebrated book *Things To Come*,[22] 1) The Roman Government, 2) Human Government, 3) Satan 4) the Church, 5) the Holy Spirit.

After listing these possibilities for the "restrainer" here are the conclusions: *The Believer's Commentary*, "The Holy Spirit indwelling the Church and individual believer seems to fit the description of the restrainer more completely and accurately than any of the others."[23] Dr. Pentecost chimes in similarly, "By mere elimination, the Holy Spirit must be the restrainer. All other suggestions fall short of meeting the requirements...."[24] Notice the speculative tone of the conclusion reached in this commentary. "The Holy Spirit indwelling the Church and individual believer *seems to fit* the description of the restrainer more completely and accurately than any of the others." The phrase "seems to fit" means it is not concrete, but implies *after considering the others, the Holy Spirit is probably the best option*." This statement is not a fact but is more of a choice by default. It cannot be over stated that vs. 6 and 7 never stated that it is the Holy Spirit who is restraining. Scholars filled in the blank with the Holy Spirit option and then built the restrainer doctrine around that concept. Therefore, it is taught as if it were fact. Now that scholars have filled in the blanks with the Holy Spirit option, this makes that interpretation a principal foundation onto which pretrib is built.

Since pretrib has declared the restrainer to be the Holy Spirit, (although Paul *does not* say that in the text), so now it is the Holy Spirit that is restraining the revealing of the man of sin (the Beast / the Antichrist). Secondly, that means the Holy Spirit must be the one to be "taken out of the way" before the Antichrist can be revealed. And since the Holy Spirit is resident in the believer and the believer is part of the body of

21 The Believer' Commentary, 2 Thessalonians 2, pg 2054
22 Things to Come, J. Dwight Pentecost, pg 259-262
23 Ibid, The Believer's Commentary
24 Things to Come, J. Dwight Pentecost, pg 262

Christ, the Church, that means, thirdly, when the restrainer is removed, the Church goes with Him, before the Antichrist is revealed. This is a principal reason why pretrib asserts that the church is gone before Daniel's 70th week, and after Revelation chapter 3. Therefore, none of what transpires in Revelation from chapter 4 through 19, applies to the church or Christians. Therefore, how 2 Thes. 2, is interpreted, has an influence on how events in Revelation are interpreted.

Pretrib proponents emphasize the point that the word *church* does not appear again in Revelation after chapter 3 until all is fulfilled. Since they interpret 2 Thes. 2 the way they do, it affects how they process the information in Revelation and Daniel. They come to Revelation with a preconceived notion that the church is already gone. The linchpin of that aspect of interpretation comes from the Holy Spirit being the restrainer of 2 Thessalonians 2. We will show that this is a monumental flaw in this widely accepted theory.

WHO IS THE BEAST?

Before we can rightly divide who is the restrainer of 2 Thessalonians 2, we first must answer the question, "Who is the Beast?" First of all, the term the beast, the Antichrist, and the man of lawlessness, or the man of sin, are all synonymous terms. In the book of Daniel, he is also called the "little horn" (Daniel 7:8). In Revelation he is called the beast, in 1st and 2nd John he is called the Antichrist. These are just a few of his names. However, there is much more to this individual than his various names. When one does a careful study, you will find that there are three different aspects of the beast. The first two consist of: (1) The Kingdom of the beast, (2) The human dictator himself and the third aspect I will cover in great detail later in this chapter. A clear understanding of the three aspects of the beast is vitally important if you are going to understand *who* and *what* is restraining the Antichrist.

In the book of Revelation there are two Greek words that are translated *beast* in English. One word is *zōon*[25] (dzo-on), which is used in reference to the four angelic creatures found in Revelation 4 (see Rev 4:7). Zōon means *a living thing*. From the word *zōon*, is where we get our English

_____
25 Strong's Greek Dictionary, *zōon*, 2226

word zoo. The other Greek word that is translated beast is *therion*[26] (they-ree-on), which refers to *a wild, venomous animal*. It is the latter term for the beast that appropriately applies to the dictator of the world's final Gentile kingdom, the Antichrist.

THE KINGDOM OF THE BEAST

In Revelation 13, John gives us a symbolic description of the beast.

> Then I stood on the sand of the sea. And I saw a beast rising up out of the sea, having seven heads and ten horns, and on his horns ten crowns, and on his heads a blasphemous name. Now the beast which I saw was like a leopard, his feet were like the feet of a bear, and his mouth like the mouth of a lion. The dragon gave him his power, his throne, and great authority.
>
> Rev. 13:1-2, also see Dan. 7:1-8, 15-28

Revelation 17 gives us the breakdown of what these symbols mean.

> Here is the mind which has wisdom. The seven heads are seven mountains on which the woman sits, and they are seven kings; five have fallen, one is, the other has not yet come; and when he comes, he must remain a little while. The ten horns which you saw are ten kings who have not yet received a kingdom, but they receive authority as kings with the beast for one hour. These have one purpose, and they give their power and authority to the beast.
>
> Revelation 17:9-10, 12-13

More information about the beast's kingdom in the following passages.

> It was also given to him to make war with the saints and to overcome them, and authority over every tribe and people and tongue and nation was given to him. All who dwell on the earth will worship him, *everyone* whose name has not been written from the foundation of the world in the book of life of the Lamb who has been slain.
>
> Revelation 13:7-8

---

26 Strong's Greek Dictionary, *therion*, 2342

> And he causes all, the small and the great, and the rich
> and the poor, and the free men and the slaves, to be given
> a mark on their right hand or on their forehead, and *he*
> *provides* that no one will be able to buy or to sell, except
> the one who has the mark, *either* the name of the beast
> or the number of his name.   Revelation 13:16-17

As we can see, the Beast's kingdom will have sweeping worldwide authority, granted by Satan, through a coalition of a ten-nation confederacy. In this one-world governmental system, everyone on earth will be under his authority. The Beast will have enormous military power, and will have total control over worldwide economics and force the world to receive his mark that without it, a person would not be able to buy or sell. These are all aspects of the kingdom of the beast.

THE HUMAN DICTATOR

The next aspect of the beast that I would like to examine is the person that will become the Beast, or the Antichrist. In Daniel 7, there are some key verses that describe the Beast's actions. Let's begin at verse 8.

> I was considering the horns, and there was another horn,
> a little one, coming up among them, before whom three
> of the first horns were plucked out by the roots. And
> there, in this horn, were eyes like the eyes of a man, and
> a mouth speaking pompous words.

In this passage, the beast is identified as being *a man* that will pluck up three of the other horns by the roots and speak arrogant things. Perhaps the uprooting of the three is in reference to some kind of political or military coup. Then at verse 25:

> He shall speak pompous words against the Most High,
> Shall persecute the saints of the Most High, And shall
> intend to change times and law. Then the saints shall be
> given into his hand for a time and times and half a time.

More information is given about this man. First of all, he will speak blasphemous things against God and make war with God's saints, killing many of them. He will also change established times and laws, which would certainly mean taking away the daily sacrifice, a condition of the seven-year covenant. However, this will include the removal of all other religious holidays, particularly Christian and Jewish holidays like Christmas, Easter, Passover, Hanukkah; and any laws that concern the worship of any God other than himself (see Dan.9:27, 2 Thes. 2:4).

And finally, we find out exactly how long he will have to do his evil bidding. The phrase used to tell us is: *time, times and the dividing of time*. The word translated *time* in this verse comes from a word of Aramaic origin *iddan*,[27] (id-dawn) which means, "a year." The word *times* means "two years" and *the dividing of time* is equal to "one-half year," totaling three-and-one-half years. This is the time frame that the Antichrist has to rule "as the beast," which coincides with the "last half" of Daniel's 70th week. Daniel's prophecy coincides with Revelation 13:5, which identifies the beast's time as forty-two months (42, 30-day months) totaling three-and-one-half years. Why is three and one-half years so significant? Because three-and-one-half years is exactly half of the seven year time period of Daniel's 70th week.

From 2 Thessalonians 2, we get more information about the human aspect of the beast:

> Let no one in any way deceive you, for *it will not come* unless the apostasy comes first, and the man of lawlessness is revealed, the son of destruction, who opposes and exalts himself above every so-called god or object of worship, so that he takes his seat in the temple of God, displaying himself as being God.
>
> 2 Thessalonians 2:3-4

The Beast, referred to here as the *man of sin* and *the son of perdition*, will walk into the Most Holy Place of the rebuilt temple and sit on the throne of God declaring himself to be God. This act coincides with the *Abomination of Desolation* of Matthew 24:15, and Daniel 9:27, 11:31. Another interesting aspect about the Antichrist is "He will show no regard for the gods of his fathers or for the desire of women..." (Daniel 11:37).

---

27 New American Standard Exhaustive Concordance of the Bible, *iddan*, 5732

The Third Aspect, the Beast from the Bottomless Pit

In Ephesians 6:12, the Apostle Paul informs us that there is more to this present world than what meets the eye. The apostle states:

> For we do not wrestle against flesh and blood, but against principalities, against powers, against the rulers of the darkness of this age, against spiritual hosts of wickedness in the heavenly places.

Here, Paul informs us about the demonic activity in the unseen spiritual realms, that insidiously influences human activity and world events. What Paul says here, we will learn, also applies to the beast. Although many very authoritative and prolific authors and scholars have written extensively on this topic, hardly any comment on the demonic aspect of the beast. Historically, the pretribulation position has not probed this aspect of the beast. Many say that it is Satan himself that possesses the beast, but the scriptures will show unequivocally that this is an error as well. In this section, I will show that a demon who is imprisoned in the abyss also known as the *bottomless pit*, plays a role in the persona of the *man of sin*, who is also known as; *the son of perdition*, the *beast*, and the *Antichrist*.

Among the first references that we see of the *beast* in Revelation in regards to the 7 heads and 10 horns symbology are found in Rev. 13:1, where he is seen as rising up from the sea. However, this character is not to be confused with the imagery found in Rev.12:3, where the scarlet colored dragon, with seven heads and ten horns, is Satan. According to the *MacArthur Commentary*, the beast rising out of the sea, is the demon rising out of the bottomless pit (see MacArthur Bible Commentary pg. 2017), whereas Walvoord says: the "sea," represents "the sea of humanity," (see *The Bible Knowledge Commentary*, pg. 960).

We are also informed that the beast will have a forty-two-month reign and that he will get his power from Satan. These are just a few of the attributes and descriptions that we get of the Antichrist. However, a passage of scripture about the beast that is normally overlooked is found in Rev. 11:7, where the passage refers to him as "the beast out of the abyss." It is this depiction of the beast that is extremely important because it is the *first mention* of his connection to the abyss. Then in Revelation 17 an angel gives greater insight into the mystery of the beast that ascends from the abyss, that was not evident in chapter thirteen.

In the book of Revelation, angels play a key role in these apocalyptic and eschatological events. This is also the case in chapter 17. In this chapter, John is having a conversation with an angel who begins to explain the secret aspects of the beast. Beginning at verse 7 the angel says: "Why did you marvel? I will tell you the *mystery* of the woman and of the beast that carries her, which has the seven heads and the ten horns." The word *mystery* comes from the Greek word *musterion*[28] that means; "the unmanifested or private counsel of God, (God's) secret, the secret thoughts, plans, and dispensations of God which are hidden from human reason, as well as from all other comprehension below the divine level, and await either fulfillment or revelation to those for whom they are intended." This is exactly what the angel does with John, he discloses the unmanifested or private counsel of God, by revealing the hidden truth about the Beast. In verse eight, the angel says:

> The beast that you saw was, and is not, and will ascend out of the bottomless pit and go to perdition. And those who dwell on the earth will marvel, whose names are not written in the Book of Life from the foundation of the world, when they see the beast that was, and is not, and yet is. (NKJV)

From this vantage point we get a very interesting view of the beast. The scriptures clearly tell us that the beast shall *ascend out of the bottomless pit* (or the Abyss). From this, it is plain that the third aspect of the beast is a demonic principality. The fact that the beast comes up from the bottomless pit, was not evident to John when he saw him rising up out of the "sea." (see Rev 13:1). This knowledge could have only come from a heavenly host, in this case an angel.

---

28 BDAG, A Greek-English Lexicon, 3466 (Strong's), *musterion,* (mystery)

WHAT IS THE BOTTOMLESS PIT?

The term *bottomless pit* comes from the Greek word, *abyssos*[29] which is translated *abyss* in modern translations. Whenever this term is used in the book of the Revelation, it's in reference to demons (see Rev. 9:1-2). Dr. Spiro Zodhiates, states that the bottomless pit, "is a prison in which evil powers are confined and out of which they can at times be released."[30] The *Greek-English Lexicon of the New Testament and Other Early Christian Literature* (BDAG), also defines the abyss "...as the abode of the Antichrist...." Also speaking of those incarcerated in the abyss, "...its inmates until their release in the tribulation before the end are the Antichrist...."[31] Therefore, the bottomless pit / abyss is a place of incarceration where demonic principalities are kept in detention.

Upon further examination of Rev. 17:8, we are given some specific information about this demon's times of involvement in the earthly realm. The angel says that the beast that John saw: *was, and is not, and will ascend out of the bottomless pit.* Then he goes on to say, and all that dwell on the earth....shall wonder, when they see the beast that *was, is not and yet is* (Rev17:7-8, KJV).

At first this passage may seem very confusing, but it actually makes a lot of sense when understood in its context. The phrase: *was, is not, and will ascend*, are three tenses of time, (past, present, and future) which are relative to John's present day. But these time frames apply to the demon. For example, the demon "was" prior to John's day and "is not" during John's day but "will ascend out of the bottomless pit" in the future beyond John's day.

From the demon's perspective he "was" active or not in the bottomless pit, prior to John's days. He "is not" while being detained in the bottomless pit during John's days, but "will ascend out of the bottomless pit," sometime in the future beyond John's days. In verse 10, we get more information that will help us understand the symbols used to describe this demon. "There are also seven kings. Five have fallen, one is, and the

29 Strong's Greek Dictionary, *abyssos, 12*
30 The Complete Word Studies Dictionary of the New Testament, Dr. Spiro Zodhiates, pg 61, abyssos/bottomless pit.
31 Kittel, Gerhard, *The Theological Dictionary of the New Testament*, Vol. 1, pg 9-10, *Abyss*

other has not yet come. And when he comes, he must continue a short time."

In this passage, the angel tells John, that there shall be seven kings or kingdoms, that shall rise on the world scene. Five of these kingdoms were already fallen, one of them was, and the other had not come yet during John's time but was going to rise later. The kingdom that was in power during John's day was Rome. It was Domitian the Emperor of Rome, that actually banished John to the island of Patmos. By this time John was well in to his nineties and the emperor probably thought he could silence the Gospel message by exiling John to an island reserved for prisoners and slaves. Domitian was probably very perturbed by the fact that John miraculously escaped execution.[32]

Being as it was, Patmos is where John received the divine Revelation. Therefore, Rome was the kingdom "that is." To get a good understanding of the five kingdoms that are fallen, we must understand that Satan has had a specific network of powerful nations. Over the centuries, the Devil has used major Gentile kingdoms bent on world domination, to persecute the nation of Israel. Although it would be God's divine providence that determined who, when, and where Israel would be persecuted for her national and moral sins, God would use Gentile nations controlled by Satan, to accomplish His will (see Habakkuk 1-3).

With this in mind, all one would have to do is read the Old Testament to discover who five of the seven heads that had already fallen by John's day are (Rev.17:10). Five great Gentile nations persecuted and ruled over Israel prior to the Romans. These were Egypt, Babylon, Medo-Persia, Greece, and Syria. Some scholars cite Assyria because it was a much greater kingdom than Syria. However, I like Syria because this was the nation of Antiochus who was a type of antichrist through the abomination of desolation. Rome was the one in power during John's day; the other kingdom had not yet come.

It is *my belief* that the seventh kingdom was Nazi-Germany under the dictatorship of Adolf Hitler. The Third Reich (German: *Drittes Reich*) denotes the Nazi state as a historical successor to the Roman Empire, under Hitler. It is quite obvious that Hitler had a great hatred for the

---

32   https://www.britannica.com/biography/Saint-John-the-Apostle (Tertullian's account)

Jews. We are all quite aware of his attempted genocide of the Jewish people where over six million were slaughtered in the Nazi death camps like Auschwitz, Sobibor, and Treblinka. In Hitler's insanity, his own genetically engineered Aryan race would rule with him after he conquered the world. At the close of World War II, when Germany was decisively defeated, on April 30, 1945, Hitler committed suicide before he could be captured and tried as a war criminal for crimes against humanity. It was just a few short years later that God fulfilled His prophecy that Israel would be gathered from among the nations and re-established in the land of Israel (Jer. 32:37, Ezek. 37:12-15).

On May 14th, 1948, God reestablished the nation of Israel in a day (Isa.66:8). He mocked Satan's attempt to use Hitler to wipe out the Jews right before God was going to fulfill the prophecy that Israel would be gathered back to her land. With Israel, being back in the Promised Land restarts the proverbial prophetic clock. John said that the seventh king when he comes, he will continue for a short time. In comparison to the other six empires seen symbolically in Rev. 17:10, Nazi-Germany and Hitler's reign was for a short time. Again, I emphasize, this is *my* belief.

THE EIGHTH KING

Now let's return to Revelation 17, beginning at verse 11, the passage says: "And the beast that was, and is not, is himself also the eighth, and is of the seven, and is going to perdition." From this passage we see that the beast that "was" and "is not" but "is himself also the eighth and is of the seven." I must concede this is another difficult passage of Scripture. However, the angel is communicating that the beast out of the bottomless pit belongs to this group of kings (the seven) and was active in one of those historic kingdoms. This is why he "was," prior to John's days, but during John's days he was already locked in the bottomless pit where he has been rendered completely inactive as though he was dead. This is why the angel told John that the beast, "is not," but in reality "yet is," and "will ascend out of the bottomless pit," in the future.

At the time this demon is released out of the bottomless pit, he will actually become the "eighth" head (Rev.17:11), in his encore appearance on the world scene. Once this ancient demon is released from the bottomless pit to rule through his human counterpart, the son of perdition, he will get another chance to persecute Israel and the saints for three-and-one-half years. Revelation 17:8 informs us that when the beast is released he goes into perdition, meaning that he goes into destruction. An interesting fact about this is in 2 Thessalonians 2:3 (KJV), the beast is called *the son of perdition*. Which one of the heads this demon possessed in the past is unknown, but it is certain he will possess the Antichrist for three-and-one-half years, the last half of Daniel's 70th week.

It is reasonable, but not proven, that since Antiochus Epiphanes IV, referred to in Daniel 11:21-35, is the one whom Jesus refers to in Matthew 24:15, as the type of antichrist to come (see Rev. 13). Therefore, if Antiochus was possessed by a demon (2 Maccabees 9:8 calls his arrogance *superhuman*[33]), then it is *possible* that it is the same demon that makes his encore appearance as the apocalyptic beast when he possesses the Antichrist. Antiochus and the Antichrist (the beast) are prophetically related because of their desecration of the temple and persecution of the Jews. Therefore, Antiochus is the official "type" of the apocalyptic Antichrist.

THE ABYSS IN THE GOSPELS AND EPISTLES

Back in the mid-90s, I enrolled in Trinity Evangelical Divinity School, to take a Revelation course being taught by the renowned scholar D. A. Carson. One of the many things he taught us about Revelation is to avoid drawing tight doctrinal boundaries around apocalyptic literature. Therefore, with that in mind, if what I am proposing is correct, I should be able to substantiate it with scriptures beyond the pages of Revelation. Therefore, let us refer to the 8th chapter of the Gospel of Luke, where Jesus has the encounter with the demoniac at Gadera.

> And Jesus asked him, saying, What is thy name? And he said, Legion: because many devils were entered into him. And they besought him that he would not command them to go out **into the deep**. And there was there an herd of many swine feeding on the mountain: and they besought him that he would suffer them to enter into them.

---

33 2 Maccabees is one of several books contained in the Apocrypha written during the intertestamental period that were not included in the Protestant bibles, but are found in certain versions of the KJV and RSV, NRSV and others. Protestant scholars do not classify the Apocrypha among the inspired writings, but do contain important historical information.

> And he suffered them. Then went the devils out of the
> man, and entered into the swine: and the herd ran vio-
> lently down a steep place into the lake, and were choked.
>   Luke 8:30-33, KJV

Here we have the account of the maniac of the Gadarenes which is also
found in Mark and Matthew. This text is interesting because it gives us
some insight from the perspective of a legion of demons. In the 28th verse
of this passage, there is an intriguing exchange between the demon(s)
and Jesus. It's not surprising that the demons knew Jesus. "When he saw
Jesus, he cried out, and fell down before him, and with a loud voice said,
What have I to do with thee, Jesus, *thou* Son of God most high? I beseech
thee, torment me not." In Matthew (8:29) this question is expanded to
"art thou come hither to torment us before the time?" Jesus' response
was, "what is your name?" The answer is astounding, "legion,[34] because
many demons had entered into him."

Immediately after being in the presence of the Lord, the demons started
pleading their case, specifically for the Lord not to command them to
go into "the deep." The deep here is *abyssos*, the abyss, the bottomless
pit, a place of confinement and torment in which the demons were well
aware. Obviously, it was not time for them to be in the abyss, so the Lord
allowed them to stay in the earth realm. After coming out of the man,
they went into a herd of swine who then drown themselves in the lake.
The subject of the abyss in relationship to demons is an established fact,
even in the gospel narratives.

FALLEN ANGELS RESTRAINED IN CHAINS

Two other references in the Epistles concerning restraint of fallen angels
or demons[35] are 2 Pet 2:4 "For if God spared not the angels that sinned,
but cast *them* down to hell, and delivered *them* into *chains of darkness*, to be
reserved unto judgment...." The second is Jude 1:6, "And the angels
which kept not their first estate, but left their own habitation, he hath
reserved in *everlasting chains* under darkness unto the judgment of the
great day."

34 a legion, numbering in the time of Augustus about 6,000 soldiers, usually with approxi-
mately an equal number of auxiliary troops. BDAG
35 Some cite a difference between the two, demons are disembodied spirits, and fallen angels
are of the angelic order.

Since angels and demons are non-corporeal beings, obviously physical chains that are familiar to humans are not what restrain demons. However, there are "chains" appropriate to restrain demons, albeit not physical ones. What these chains actually consist of is not the principal issue. The point is these beings can be restrained by a means appropriate for them. From the confines of the Abyss, demons are released for service in the satanic sphere here on earth and in the lower heavenly realms for specific amounts of time (more on this point later). Another reference to restrained principalities is found in Revelation 9:14, where this text speaks of angels being "bound (or restrained) in the river Euphrates" needing to be *loosed*.

From these passages, we have established that fallen angels or demonic principalities can all be contained, restrained and confined. Additionally, we established a strong connection between the beast and the abyss. Without the information given in Rev. 17:7-8, you cannot rightly understand what is "holding down" and "restraining" the manifestation and the revealing of the Antichrist.

Consider this, isn't it reasonable that when answering the question of what is restraining the revealing of the Antichrist, to at least consider the information given to us in Revelation? Is it not explicit, that the beast ascends from the abyss, a place of incarceration for demonic principalities? Why would scholars create an entire restrainer doctrine and leave out this information? As we continue in this study, we will discover that the restrainer interpretation plays a key role in the disposition of the Church and the timing of the rapture.

When it comes to Bible prophecy, we can know what has been prophesied but how it will play out in real time is always a mystery. Whenever we attempt to choreograph God's prophetic moves, as history has shown, we will be out of step with actual fulfillment. Bible teachers and scholars should never build people's hopes on speculation and things they cannot prove. However, they should be honest and inform people of the Biblical options and not merely focus upon doctrines that complement their traditions.

5

THE RESTRAINING MINISTRY OF ANGELS

The connection between the Abyss as being a prison for demons and or fallen angels is simply undeniable. However, the most explicit example of this is the binding of Satan.

> Then I saw an angel coming down from heaven, holding the key of the abyss and a great chain in his hand. And he laid hold of the dragon, the serpent of old, who is the devil and Satan, and bound him for a thousand years; and he threw him into the abyss, and shut *it* and sealed *it* over him, so that he would not deceive the nations any longer, until the thousand years were completed; after these things he must be released for a short time...When the thousand years are completed, Satan will be released from his prison.
>
> Revelation 20:1-3, 7

There are many aspects of this passage that deserve attention. First, the prominent character of this passage is one *unnamed* angel, not Michael. Secondly, he is coming down from heaven. This certainly implies that he is a holy angel. Thirdly, the angel is holding *the key* to the abyss. The key implies that the abyss is a locked and escape proof place of detention. Fourthly, the angel accosts, apprehends, and restrains Satan with the chain he was holding. Fifthly, the angel threw Satan into the abyss, closed up the abyss and set a containment seal over him so that Satan's powers to deceive the nations would be totally disrupted. Finally, in verse 7, after the one-thousand years is up, Satan will be released from his *prison*. The term *prison* is interesting because it leaves no doubt as to the purpose of the abyss. It is a locked prison for angelic / demonic principalities and powers.

The word *angel* comes from the Greek word *angelos* and the Hebrew word *mal-awk*, both meaning, "messenger" or "angel." Angelic beings are supernatural spirits, and constitute a distinct order, and are among the upper echelons of supernatural, created beings. Angels are immortal and are usually accredited with human characteristics, but go far beyond anything we as humans can imagine about them. Since they are not procreated, each one is a unique angelic creation, which are probably no two that are alike. Their supernatural traits are strength, immense power, and wisdom. Since angels cannot die or be destroyed, one warring angel alone could probably destroy the entire population of the earth. Second Kings 19:35, is an example of angelic power. In one night, a single angel killed 185,000 soldiers before dawn.

Angels carry out numerous tasks throughout the universe and on the earth. They are an innumerable multitude that go about doing the bidding of God and fall into two categories; God's holy angels and the devil and his angels or demons. Another very interesting fact is, *in the Bible*, angels are never referred to as children, and are never referred to in the *feminine* but are always referred to in the masculine gender where the typical pronouns used for them are: *man, him, he and his.*[36]

Some other duties angels are tasked with are encamping around the saints of God, and serving the heirs of salvation (Job 1:10, Ps.34:7, Heb.1:14). Strengthening weakened human beings and encouraging them (Luke 22:43, Acts 27:23-24). Fighting for and protecting humans with inconceivable destructive powers (Ex.23:20, 2 Kings 6:17 2 Kings 19:35). Overseeing and affecting atmospheric conditions, celestial bodies, and wildlife (Rev. 7:1, 16:8, 19:17) and even ruling over entire nations (Dan. 10-12). These are just a few of their known duties. There is also a hierarchy among angels, *Angel of the Lord*, (usually the presence of deity in angelic form) *Archangel* (Michael, also called a *chief prince* (Dan. 10:13), *Cherub, Cherubim, Seraphim* (among the host of winged angels, associated with being in the presence of God and worship).

Understanding all of what we have covered so far concerning angels and the abyss, the facts are: if Satan himself can be bound, gagged, and restrained with chains, then cast into the bottomless pit for a predeter-

36 Holman Illustrated Bible Dictionary, *Angels*

mined amount of time, *so can any other demon*. If Satan can be rendered completely powerless by setting a seal on him, *so can any other demon*. If Satan can be locked in the bottomless pit, without the chance of escape, *so can any other demon*. If Satan must be released before he can leave the bottomless pit, *so must any other demon*. This is the same bottomless pit that *the beast* must ascend out from, a place referred as a *prison*. It is highly unlikely that the beast is receiving any special privileges. I seriously doubt that the beast has his own key to the bottomless pit and can come and go as he pleases.

It is clear; before demons go into the abyss they are restrained with chains by the angels. Before they come out of the bottomless pit, they must go past the angel that holds the key to the bottomless pit, and their restraints must be removed. God determines when these demons are to be locked up and gives the order according to His own purposes. So, the authority comes from God, just as a Judge may order a bench warrant for a particular criminal. The Judge gives the authority to a deputy to pick him up, arrest and detain him until his trial date comes where he will then be sentenced. Similarly, so it is with God and his angels. God, the Holy Spirit *does not* personally restrain demons. This is a function wholly assigned to angels just as a judge does not personally restrain, incarcerate, and maintain a criminal he has sentenced.

The reason we must consider the angels as tactical agents of restraint is because of where the beast is being held. This is not just an ideological or conceptual argument; this is a necessary argument because the beast *ascends out of the abyss*. So, you *must* factor these biblical realities into the equation when making a determination on what is restraining the revealing of the Antichrist from the 2 Thessalonian 2 perspective. Not using this information when making that determination is simply wrong and biblically and hermeneutically irresponsible. Here is what is stated in the *Theological Dictionary of the New Testament*, concerning the restrainer and speaking of the usages of *katecho* (kat-ekh'-o) the restrainer found in 2 Thes. 2:6-7:

> It is also used in a bad sense of holding illegally, holding in prison. Rather along the same lines it means to prevent an evil person or power from breaking out, (as one

imprisons criminals to protect society against them)....
The mysterious ungodly force which will be let loose just
before the end, the mystery of iniquity, takes concrete
shape in a *anthropos* and therefore the *katecho* (who does
not have to be a historical magnitude and might be an
angel) is a concrete manifestation of restraint.[37]

Dr. Kiddle and Bromiley's commentary is an unbiased critical exegesis
on the uses on the term *katecho*, (the restrainer of 2 Thes. 2:6-7) that
cannot be ignored. Their assessment of the 2 Thes. 2 texts, clearly sees
the possibility that the restrainer can be of an angelic nature.

BACK TO THE PRETRIB ARGUMENT

We have already examined who pretrib says the restrainer is. According
to their position, it's unequivocally the Holy Spirit. So, let's examine
the scriptures *they used* to back up that theory. Remember, they provided
a list of who they or others historically have said who the restrainer is
and gave reasons why those couldn't fit the bill. But now let's examine
what scriptures they do use to support the Holy Spirit restrainer concept.
Once again, we will use the *Believer's Commentary*, page 2054, but these
are the same scriptures that other pretrib proponents use as well.[38]

Genesis 6:3

And the LORD said, My spirit shall not always strive with man, for
that he also *is* flesh: yet his days shall be an hundred and twenty years
(KJV).

> *Response*: It is difficult to see how you get a Holy Spirit restraining
> ministry example from this passage. In 2 Thes. 2:6-7, the restrainer is
> *holding back*, preventing the Antichrist from being revealed. In Gene-
> sis 6, God is not *holding back* sinners from sinning. The operative word
> in this passage is "strive." The NIV translates it as "contend." Con-
> tending with someone is different than *restraining* someone. The fact

---

37 Theological Dictionary of the New Testament, vol. II, pp 829-830, *katecho*
38 Numerous pretribulationist cite the same, or variations of the passages listed in the Believer's Commentary. MacArthur, New Testament Commentary, 2 Thes.2, pg 278, Walvoord, Bible
Knowledge Commentary, 2 Thes. 2, pg 719, Dwight Pentecost, Things To Come, pg 262, Norman Geisler, Systematic Theology vol. 4, pg 616

that a person *is contending* implies they are able to resist. A restrained person *cannot* contend or resist because they are *prohibited from doing so*.

If God restrained the people in Noah's day, He wouldn't have had to flood the world because they would have been prevented from sinning. Therefore, God didn't *restrain* them, He *contended* with them at least to some degree through Noah's preaching (2 Peter 2:5), as an appeal to repent which they clearly ignored. There was no physical restraint exerted upon them. For example, a person that has the freedom to escape can ignore a police order not to run. However, the officer can ensure they stay put by placing them in handcuffs and leg irons shackled to the floor. That's restraint! Sorry, this Scripture does not support a restraining ministry of the Holy Spirit.

John 14:26
But the Comforter, *which is* the Holy Ghost, whom the Father will send in my name, **he** shall teach you all things, and bring all things to your remembrance, whatsoever I have said unto you. John 14:26 (KJV)

> *Response*: Pretrib uses this passage because the Holy Spirit is being referred to using the masculine pronoun "he." The point they are making is that Paul used "he" as well when he spoke of the restrainer.

John 15:26
But when the Comforter is come, whom I will send unto you from the Father, *even* the Spirit of truth, which proceedeth from the Father, **he** shall testify of me: John 15:26 (KJV)

> *Response*: Once again, the masculine pronoun "he" is used. Nothing here about restraining the world's sin. As a matter of fact, it's getting worse! Because of the increase of wickedness, the love of most will grow cold (Matthew 24:12, NIV). Speaking of the perilous times of the last days Paul declares, "But evil men and impostors will proceed from bad to worse, deceiving and being deceived" (2 Timothy 3 3:13).

John 16:7-11
Nevertheless I tell you the truth; It is expedient for you that I go away: for if I go not away, the Comforter will not come unto you; but if I depart, I will send **him** unto you. And when **he** is come, **he** will reprove the world of sin, and of righteousness, and of judgment: Of sin, because they be-

lieve not on me; Of righteousness, because I go to my Father, and ye see me no more; Of judgment, because the prince of this world is judged. (KJV)

Response: Once again, the masculine pronoun "he" is used. However, the NIV translates it this way. "When he comes, he will prove the world to be in the wrong about sin and righteousness and judgment." This is not an act of restraining sin. This time masculine pronouns "he and him" are used, *him* once and *he* twice. Convicting, or proving the world wrong about sin, is quite different than restraining the world from sinning. Where does the Bible show the Holy Spirit restraining someone in the act of sinning, or someone that wanted to sin being blocked from sinning by the Holy Spirit?

1 John 4:4
Ye are of God, little children, and have overcome them: because greater is **he** that is in you, than **he** that is in the world. 1 John 4:4 (KJV)

Response: masculine pronoun "he" is used and because the Holy Spirit within the believer is greater than the Satanic force in the world. However, there is nothing here about believers being able to restrain sin in the world nor the Antichrist himself. Believers cannot restrain their own sin in the church, let alone in the world.

Isaiah 59:19b, KJV
So shall they fear the name of the LORD from the west, and his glory from the rising of the sun. When the enemy shall come in like a flood, the Spirit of the LORD shall **lift up a standard** against him.

Response: This one is interesting. The phrase "lift up a standard" comes from the Hebrew word *nus*.[39] Nus (noos) or *lift up a standard*, does not mean "physical restraint." In order to eisogete that interpretation into this text, you have to do so using the King James Version, because other versions do not support that idea at all. For example,

Isaiah 59:19b, NIV
From the west, people will fear the name of the LORD, and from the rising of the sun, they will revere his glory. For he will come like a pent-up flood that the breath of the LORD drives along.

39 Strong's Hebrew Dictionary, Lift up a standard, 5127

Isaiah 59:19b, NASB

So they will fear the name of the LORD from the west And His glory from the rising of the sun, For He will come like a rushing stream Which the wind of the LORD drives.

> *Response*: When we read about "lifting up a standard" what comes to mind is that the Holy Spirit is becoming some type of spiritual bulwark. Though that is an interesting concept, the passage does not actually bear that out. Here relying on the King James rendering does the pretrib interpreter a disservice. The imagery that would convey what the prophet is saying would be more like the wind forcefully driving something along. In either case, this is figurative language.

We have just examined the proof text that pretrib uses to back the idea of the Holy Spirit's restraining ministry. Remember, pretrib insists that Paul must be implying that it is the Holy Spirit in 2 Thes. 2:6-7 that is the restrainer. Therefore, they have set forth the passages we just covered to flush out that concept biblically. But my response to these passages being used is, "is this all they have?" These scriptural references are totally inadequate to make that case on the following basis.

1. None of these scriptures have anything to do with the Antichrist.

2. None of these scriptures have anything to do with end-time prophecy.

3. None of these scriptures have anything to do with the restraining of the Antichrist.

4. None of these scriptures have anything to do with apocalyptic literature or the book of Revelation.

5. None of these scriptures *in their context* actually prove that the Holy Spirit is the restrainer of 2 Thes. 2.

6. All of these so-called proof texts have to do with the Spirit in its role and interaction with humans. However, the removal of the restrainer is dealing with the restraint of a demonic principality making this an evil angel versus holy angel conflict (See chapter 10, *The Holy Spirit is our Helper*). Therefore the pretribulationist has employed a *collapsing*

context to reach a conclusion based upon passages that have nothing to do with what Paul was describing in 2 Thes. 2:6-7.

Historically, several commentators before and during Darby's time did not share the Holy Spirit restrainer interpretation. John Calvin states, "That Christ must enlighten the whole world by his gospel in order that the impiety of men might be the more fully attested and demonstrated. This therefore, was the delay, until the career of the gospel should be completed..." (see *Calvin's Commentary* on 2 Thes. 2:6, published in 1548).

Matthew Poole's Commentary of the Bible published in 1685, gives a synopsis of both "popish and protestant" expositors who give varying aspects of why it's Rome that is in view as the restrainer.

The Full Matthew Henry Commentary published in 1706, "There was something that hindered or withheld, or let, until it was taken away. This is supposed to be the power of the Roman empire, which the Apostle did not think fit to mention more plainly at the time...."

John Gill's Expositor, published in 1809, opted for the "Roman emperors must keep their place and dignity to prevent his appearance sooner..."(2 Thes. 2:6 note).

Barnes New Testament Notes, published in 1885 "The most natural interpretation is that which refers to civil power..."

Jamison, Fausett, Brown Commentary published in 1871, states "Romanism, as a forerunner of Antichrist, was thus kept in check by the Roman emperor...."

Robertson's New Testament Word Picture, published in 1845 "the man of lawlessness is the imperial line with its rage for deification and that of the Jewish state was the restraining power."

Adam Clarke's Commentary published in 1810-1826, "...must be some time before he could be brought forth; there was some obstacle that hindered his appearing. What this was we cannot determine with absolute certainty at so great a distance of time; but if we may rely upon the concurrent testimony of the fathers, it was the Roman empire."

John Wesley Commentary Explanatory Notes upon the New Testament published in 1753, "The power of the Roman emperors. When this is taken away, the wicked one will be revealed."

The Restrainer Rabbit Hole

What is abundantly clear is that Darby's views on the restrainer was a departure from what other scholars before and after his day believed. F.F. Bruce, records a response to a historic restrainer option when Darby writes[40]

> "the thing which restrained then is not that which restrains now. Then it was, in one sense, the Roman empire, as the fathers thought....; At present the hindrance is still the existence of the governments established by God in the world; and God will maintain them as long as there is here below the gathering of His church. Viewed in this light, the hindrance is, at the bottom, the presence of the church and of the Holy Spirit on the earth."[41]

Here, Bruce cites Darby's response to John Chrysostom, bishop of Constantinople (407 A.D.), suggestion of the Roman Empire restrainer. Surprisingly, Darby concludes that it may have been the Roman Empire in the past, but now, it's *the presence of the Church and the Holy Spirit on the earth.* However, that's Darby's conclusion, not a biblical fact. Darby initiated his foundational restrainer concept by an unsubstantiated determination. Since then, dispensationalists have sought to flush out that concept by stringing together unrelated passages to make that point.

The primary reason pretribulationist uses the Scriptures that they do to is because it is the closest they can come to developing that "concept." However, they did so without having any explicit texts directly connected to the Antichrist himself. Therefore, this is the wrong pursuit, because the restraint of evil in general or conceptually is not the focus of 2 Thessalonians 2. The passage at hand, is directing its focus to eschatological events that precede the Day of the Lord, specifically, the falling away, and the abomination of desolation, when the man of sin sits on the throne of God, declaring himself to be God.

40 F.F Bruce, Word Biblical Commentary Volume 45, pg 171
41Darby, J. N. "Notes on the Epistles to the Thessalonians." In Collected Writings, Eds. W. Kelly. London: Morrish, 1867–1900, xxvii, 437–455. Word Biblical Commentary - 1, 2 Thessalonians: Volume 45

Though it is true that Paul identifies the "mystery of iniquity" that was already working in his day, however, that by itself, does not support the idea that the Holy Spirit is the specific restrainer of the antichrist of 2 Thessalonians 2. In fact, since the mystery of iniquity was at work, itself is an indication that the mystery of iniquity cited in the passage, was not under restraint or how else could it be "working."

If God fully restrained evil, then there could be no manifestation of evil. The fact the evil persists and is getting worse, particularly in the last days, constitutes a fulfillment of prophecy whereby God is executing his sovereign prerogative to permit evil to get progressively worse. To that extent, the Holy Spirit is not preventing evil from getting worse, because God is permitting evil to run its appointed course. Therefore, if you give the Holy Spirit the role of restraining evil, for the sake of 2 Thessalonians 2 text, you are also forced to have the Holy Spirit restraining the evil the Father has permitted to operate. Is God hindering Himself? Of course not! The fact that evil exists is proof that God has a good purpose for evil., therefore it must run it's course. Dr. Norman Geisler observes:

> God knows a good purpose for all evil, even if we do not. Simply because finite minds cannot conceive of a good purpose for some evil does not mean that there is none. Since God is omniscient, he knows everything. And since he is omnibenevolent, he has a good purpose for everything.[42]

Another point to be considered here is, when you make the Holy Spirit the restrainer of evil based on 2 Thessalonians 2, you make the Holy Spirit the ineffective restrainer of evil because iniquity continuously abounds. This is an inescapable dilemma. If as 1 John 4:4 states, "greater is he that is in you than he that is in the world," supports the idea that the Holy Spirit is the restrainer, then why is evil getting worse? Why then cannot the believer through the indwelling Spirit restrain the evil that is in the world, or that exist in the church?

Therefore, it is this author's contention that this *was not* Paul's intention in the first place. When Paul wrote 2 Thessalonians 2:6-7, he only had in mind the restraint of a specific individual, the revealing of the Antichrist, who

---

42 Norman Geisler, Baker Encyclopedia of Christian Apologetics, *The Problem of Evil,* pg 222

was only to be revealed "in *his* time" (2 Thes. 2:6) in association with the day of the Lord. Paul did not have all evil for all ages in mind. By the pretribulationist expanding this concept to a historical reality, they do so beyond the intent of the passage to reinforce Darby's restrainer interpretation.

How is it that the Holy Spirit can restrain the Antichrist, but didn't restrain the evil Dylann Roof would perpetrate when he slaughtered 9 innocent Christians during Bible study, at Emmanuel A.M.E. Church, in Charleston, S.C. Not to mention other church shootings in America. The point here is, making the Holy Spirit the restrainer of evil, causes more questions than answers. Yes, the Holy Spirit implores and convicts not to sin, but He does not literally restrain or stop anyone from sinning, because sin is an act of human choice.

If passages such as Genesis 6:3, are used to make a restrainer point, (which I believe is not a good text to prove that point), then the Holy Spirit is ineffective in restraining evil because men clearly ignored the Spirit and continued their evil to the point of God destroying the world with the flood.

What the pretribulationists functionally call restraint actually boils down to the Spirit convicting of sin as in one of their proof text John 16:8 informs. However, in 2 Thessalonians 2, conviction is not what's holding the Antichrist down. Conviction by nature is passive and does not place literal restrains on anyone or anything. Neither is the Holy Spirit some *Star Trek* force-field that blocks evil or physically prevents someone from doing something sinful. The Holy Spirit's conviction of sin serves more as an inner witness that what a person is doing is wrong. Through the conscience God has made people aware of their actions. Therefore, they experience guilt. It is true that a guilty conscience can make you rethink doing something wrong, but that's not the same thing as being restrained.

However, when it comes to the demonic aspect of the Antichrist, he is literally being held down in a place called "a prison," where holy angels do the actual restraining. This is not conceptual. This is literal restraint and explicit in the Scriptures. However, pretrib used none of these passages in the formulation of their theories and thereby have failed to rightly divide the Word of Truth in this matter. Brothers and sisters, that's shameful. How could they not tell the whole story when the Scriptures about the beast and the bottomless pit have been there all the time?

6

THE WOODS/PENTECOST CHALLENGE

In the summer of 1996, I relocated to Dallas Texas. While there, I could not pass up the opportunity to reach out to Dr. John Walvoord, Chancellor of Dallas Theological Seminary (DTS). Our first contact was a telephone conversation where I requested to send him a paper based on my book *Unlocking the Door: A Key to Biblical Prophecy*, published by Huntington House, in 1994. My book, as well as my paper, cited a major flaw in the pretribulational rapture theory. Dr. Walvoord was gracious and obliged me to send my work to him for review and critique. The paper that I submitted to Walvoord, I had already submitted to Dr. D. A. Carson a year earlier while attending Trinity Evangelical Divinity School extension, (Elmbrook Study Center, Brookfield Wi.). The grade I received from Dr. Carson was an A-. He wrote on the top of the paper "Very gifted work." In 1997, I then sent a follow-up paper to Dwight Pentecost, also of DTS, based on the same premises found in the paper that D. A. Carson and Walvoord reviewed. The following is an excerpt from the paper that was sent to Pentecost:

> If one could disqualify, disprove or discredit a major tenet of any espoused theory, it may very well diminish or destroy that theory's validity. If when formulating any given hypothesis, if you fail to examine all obvious, relevant and available factors, the suppositions and conclusions derived from such an incomplete investigation, are inherently faulty and will inevitably lead to flawed conclusions. Consequently, the integrity of such a theory is compromised and its foundation could collapse under the weight of critical analysis and scrutiny.

In view of the above stated proposition, major tenets of the pretribulation rapture theory could possibly fall into the category of flawed. This theory is supported by faulty propositions and conclusions which can be attributed to a failure to factor in all obvious, relevant, and available biblical facts. One of the most critically flawed propositions in pretribulationism is the necessary and emphatic reliance on the, "He" and the "What" of 2 Thessalonians 2, being that of the Holy Spirit Himself.

The viability of this theory, heavily *but not totally*, depends on interpreting the Holy Spirit as the only capable agent of restraint, which according to 2 Thessalonians 2, is to be taken out of the way. It therefore becomes the necessary interpretation which is affirmed by numerous scholars that hold this view and serves as a cornerstone passage that backs this theory. Concerning the importance of 2 Thes. 2 in supporting pretrib theory, John Walvoord asserts:

> If, therefore, the restrainer of 2 Thessalonians 2 be identified as the Holy Spirit, another evidence is produced to indicate the translation of the church before the final tribulation period will begin on earth. While in the realm of debatable conclusions if left unsupported by other scriptural evidence, it constitutes a confirmation of the teaching that the church will be translated before the Tribulation.[43]

Let's address the pretribulation straw man argument. In order to do so I must refer to Dr. Pentecost's famous reference work entitled: *Things to Come*. In his book, Dr. Pentecost mounts a seemingly insurmountable case for the Holy Spirit only, restraining force of 2 Thessalonians 2. Before he states his case, he first refutes the historic attempts to identify the restraining force, and does an impeccable job. The following is a brief of the arguments that Dr. Pentecost uses to defend the restraining ministry of the Holy Spirit, that is found on page 262, of *Things to Come*, quoting from Gerald Stanton's work, *Kept From the Hour*[44], Dr. Pentecost asserts:

1) By mere elimination, the Holy Spirit must be the restrainer. All other suggestions fall short of meeting the requirements.

---

43   The Rapture Question, first edition, John Walvoord, pg 81
44   Kept from the Hour, Gerald Stanton, pg 110

2) The wicked one is a personality, and his operations include the realm of the supernatural. The restrainer must likewise be a personality and a spiritual being... to hold Antichrist in check until the time for his revealing. Mere agencies or impersonal spiritual forces would be inadequate.

3) To achieve all that is to be accomplished, the restrainer must be a member of the Godhead. He must be stronger than the Man of Sin and stronger than Satan who energizes him. In order to restrain evil down through the course of the age, the restrainer must be eternal... The theater of sin is the entire world: therefore, it is imperative that the restrainer be one who is not limited by time or space.

The above stated propositions are aspects of what I call a straw man argument. Here, pretrib constructs an argument built on false premises that, if left uncontested, makes the Holy Spirit interpretation the only viable restrainer. However, if there is another biblical option that is relevant and explicit, how badly would aspects of the pretrib rapture theory, as we know it, be undermined? The fact is, if there is another viable biblical interpretation, then a chain reaction of questions and doubts begins to move throughout other significant tenets of the theory that tracks back to how portions of the book of Revelation is interpreted in regards to the Church.

Since the Apostle Paul *does not* identify the restraining force of 2 Thessalonians 2, hermeneutically we are compelled to fill in the blanks. When the pretribulationist fills in the blanks, they use theological propositions and conjecture to support their theory. Additionally, when it comes to the identification of the restraining force of 2 Thessalonians 2, as we have examined, pretrib relies heavily upon indirect scriptural references unrelated to apocalyptic literature, eschatology, the book of Revelation or the Antichrist.

If there were no other viable candidates for the restrainer, this would be fine. However, what if there is another restraining force in the Bible, one would be forced to ask how it could have been missed all this time? At that question I am most baffled.

We have already covered that there are three aspects of the beast: (1) the kingdom of the beast. (2) the human monarch or dictator himself. (3) the demon that shall ascend out of the bottomless pit. Without understanding this, you cannot interpret 2 Thessalonians properly, especially without including the third aspect of the beast. This is the aspect of the beast that has been overlooked since Darby introduced this doctrine to America in the early 1800s. As stated explicitly, the beast ascends from the Abyss (Rev. 17:8). The relevance and purpose of the bottomless pit / abyss is emphasized in the following passage.

> Then I saw an angel coming down from heaven, having the key to the bottomless pit and a great chain in his hand. He laid hold of the dragon, that serpent of old, who is the Devil and Satan, and bound him for a thousand years; and he cast him into the bottomless pit, and shut him up, and set a seal on him, so that he should deceive the nations no more till the thousand years were finished. But after these things he must be released for a little while.... When the thousand years are completed, Satan will be released from his prison.
>
> Rev. 20:1-3,7 KJV

Let us compare what this passage explicitly declares against Dr. Pentecost's assertions:

1) Pentecost: By mere elimination, the Holy Spirit must be the restrainer. All other suggestions fall short of meeting the requirements.

Response: First of all, Dr. Pentecost begins his argument with a faulty premise. He eliminated the historical options for the restrainer, but he did not consider the biblical option. Rev. 20:1-3 and other passages in both the Old and New Testaments show that angels are more than capable, and do in fact restrain, in particular, even the devil himself (Dan. 10:13, Rev. 12:8-9). The fact that pretrib theorist did not include angels as possible restrainers, starts the theory off under the false pretense that all possible options for the restrainer had already been eliminated. This is a major misstep. In order to maintain a credible theory, one must examine and rule out all the relevant possibilities, or you simply have not covered all the bases. Angels who typically play a major role in apocalyptic literature are explicit biblical agents of restraint that have clearly been overlooked or intentionally left out of Dr. Pentecost's and other's assertions and conclusions.

2) Pentecost: The wicked one is a personality, and his operations include the realm of the supernatural. The restrainer must likewise be a personality and a spiritual being... to hold Antichrist in check until the time for his revealing. Mere agencies or impersonal spiritual forces would be inadequate.

Response: Angels are indeed spiritual beings, therefore are personalities, who operate in both physical and spiritual realms. Though their names are largely unknown to humans, they are in fact referred to in the masculine gender. If a single angel can restrain Satan himself, which is clear in Rev. 20:1-3, then restraining a Satanic subordinate as the beast is of no consequence. Holding the beast that ascends out of the abyss in check until the time of his counterpart's (the Antichrist) revealing is not problematic either. That is the purpose for the bottomless pit. It is a prison for demons; therefore, it holds wicked powers in check without the possibility of being breached.

3) Pentecost: To achieve all that is to be accomplished, the restrainer must be a member of the Godhead. He must be stronger than the Man of Sin and stronger than Satan who energizes him. In order to restrain evil down through the course of the age, the restrainer must be eternal... The theater of sin is the entire world: therefore, it is imperative that the restrainer be one who is not limited by time or space.

Response: Each one of these assertions is patently incorrect. In Rev. 20, the angel restrained Satan himself, the apex of evil. Though the restrainer here is a holy angel, he is certainly not a member of the Godhead. Insisting that the restrainer be a member of the Godhead was clearly an attempt to overstate the position when there was no biblical or theological basis to do so. There is a serious ontological disparity between God Almighty the supreme being and Satan a contingent angelic being. To imply that only a member of the Godhead can restrain a finite angelic being, or their activity is untenable and inappropriate and gives Satan way too much authority. Statements like this are outwardly authoritative, but they are theologically baseless.

Secondly, in Rev. 12, Michael and his angels fought against the devil and his angels and that text explicitly declares that "Satan was not strong enough" (NIV), for Michael's angelic army. This is a direct contradiction to Dr. Pentecost's assertion, because he said that only a member of the Godhead is strong enough. Clearly, angels are indeed *strong enough* to restrain Satan because they threw the devil and his angels out of heaven. Additionally, though angels are immortal they are not *eternal*, because they are created, contingent and finite beings. Dr. Pentecost's position necessitates that only an eternal being could qualify as the restrainer. Once again, this point is inaccurate because eternality is clearly not necessary. The angels opposing Satan only needed to be present since the time of the heavenly rebellion where sin originated. There is no basis to suggest that evil exist eternally. Prior to the heavenly rebellion, there was no manifestation of evil and after the new heaven and new earth comes, other than in the lake of fire, there will be no evil.

In addition to that, holy angels are numerous enough to counter Satan's army. This is at least implied in the Rev. 12:4 text, where Satan drew only a third of the angels. Therefore, holy angels out number Satan's angels on a two-to-one ratio, and many of the ungodly angels are imprisoned, further reducing their ranks. And as evidenced in scripture, two angels can be involved with demonic principalities (Dan 10:13). Theoretically, no matter where in the universe, whether in the physical or spiritual realms, there are enough holy angels to check, or literally oppose demonic forces at any time or any place. So at least from a tactical numerical aspect, holy angels can stop any campaign the devil and his angels could attempt.

Pretribulationists, once again, have presented a straw man argument. They first build a seemingly impregnable theological position by reporting to have examined and eliminated all the possibilities as related to the restrainer. However, in this discussion, at each one of the points in Dr. Pentecost's arguments above, there were clear and explicit scriptures (not theological arguments) to show a definitive and decisive biblical text to contradict each point. Again, I emphasize, that I countered each of their assertions with Scripture, not philosophical or doctrinal concepts.

It must be noted, if the Holy Spirit is not the restrainer of 2 Thes.2, then one cannot use that text to support a pretribulational rapture, because under those circumstances you do not have the removal of the Holy Spirit before the revealing of the Antichrist. With this understanding, pretrib does not lose the game, but it's a major chip taken off the table.

7
PROVIDENTIAL AND TACTICAL RESTRAINT

According to Colossians 1:17, all things are held together by God. Providentially, God controls all things, but an important distinction to be made here is, *God does not do all things*, and this is a point that many pretrib scholars do not factor into their theories. For example, on May 1, 2011, President Obama gave orders to his military commanders to kill Osama bin Laden. Our highly trained *Seal Team Six* flew into Pakistan, led a stealthy raid on bin Laden's compound where they valiantly terminated him. Afterward, they removed his body from the compound and buried him at sea in the Indian Ocean. President Obama issued the executive order, but it was the *Seal Team Six* who were the tactical assets that completed the mission. Even if he was qualified to do so, no one would expect the President to carry out that raid himself. The President of the United States does not partake in military operations. He gives the order, but his tactical assets carry it out.

The soldiers on the ground are doing the fighting. It is the doing aspect that must be considered when determining who is the restrainer of 2 Thessalonians 2. God's judicial or providential restraint is not what's in focus in 2 Thes. 2:6-7, because *something* and *someone* that's restraining has to be removed. Subsequently, that makes this a *tactical* issue not a *conceptual* issue. Therefore, in order to solve the mystery of the restrainer, you must factor in the information from Revelation 17:8, that reveals there is a demonic aspect of the beast who is literally locked-up. The beast may be there because of judicial authority, but tactical restraint is what's actually keeping him there. Just as a judge can order a criminal to be imprisoned, the judge's order will not keep the prisoner from trying to break out or escape. The tactical angelic assets carry out the functionary role of keeping the Antichrist principality in check until it's time for him to be loosed from the abyss. God Himself in the person of the Holy Spirit does not have to carry out this role personally, just as President Obama didn't personally go to Pakistan to kill bin Laden, even though he gave the order under his authority. You must understand that pretribulationism has wrongly created a necessity that *only* the Holy Spirit can restrain Satan, and by extension, the revealing of the Antichrist. Revelation 17:8 and 20:1-3, clearly refutes this assertion.

Before we examine some Biblical examples of tactical angelic restraint of demonic forces, I would like to emphasize the point that God does not do everything in another way. For example, the preaching of the gospel and keys to the kingdom of heaven, by way of preaching was committed to men. When the Apostle Paul, (then Saul of Tarsus) was confronted by the resurrected Lord, on the road to Damascus, why didn't Jesus save Paul on the spot? Think about it. Isn't it the Lord the one who actually saves souls? Isn't it the Lord who redeems? Isn't it the Lord who died on the cross? Isn't it the Lord whose blood was shed? Isn't it the Lord who rose again from the dead? Isn't it the Lord whose body is the Church, which He is also the head? Obviously, the answer to these questions are, yes.

However, why didn't Jesus simply say, "I'm the Lord. I am He who saves. Confess me as Lord and I'll save you now." Certainly, the Lord could have said this. But why didn't he? The answer is simple. He could have, but this was not the order that He instituted for men to be saved. The Lord chose the foolishness of preaching to save them that are lost. The gospel message, and belief in Christ through the preaching of the gospel is how the Lord chose to save people (1 Cor. 1:21, Eph. 3:6). The resurrected Christ does not preach the Gospel! Preaching was committed to men to do, not the Lord. Therefore, even though Christ could have saved Paul on the spot, he told Paul to go to Ananias, and he would tell Paul what to do (Acts 9:1-18). Christ controls all things, but He does not do all things.

Our next example comes from a charge that Peter makes against the Jews concerning the crucifixion of Christ. The apostle declares, "This man was handed over to you by *God's deliberate plan and foreknowledge*; and *you, with the help of wicked men*, put him to death by nailing him to the cross

(Acts 2:23, NIV). Once again, we have an amazing testament of God sovereign providence at work. God was in control of bringing Christ into the world specifically to die for the sin of the world. By His *deliberate plan and foreknowledge* (determinate counsel and foreknowledge, KJV) Christ was crucified exactly as the Father ordained, yet *by the hands of godless men* (NASB) they put him to death. God controls all things, but God does not do all things. It can never be said that the Father crucified Christ; even though providentially He was in control through His deliberate plan. God didn't do it. "Wicked men" were the responsible agents that crucified Christ. Paul declares, "None of the rulers of this age understood it, for if they had, they would not have crucified the Lord of glory" (1 Corinthians 2:8, NIV).

Our final example we must consider the actions of Judas Iscariot. The Scriptures are clear, "For the Son of Man is to go just as it is written of Him; but woe to that man by whom the Son of Man is betrayed! It would have been good for that man if he had not been born" (Mark 14:21). Clearly, God's providence was emphasized by the statement, "as it is written." In other words, events concerning Christ's betrayal and death will unfold exactly as God has predetermined.

In Zech. 11:12-13, the prophecy about Jesus' betrayal is explicit, down to the amount (30 pieces) and the type of currency (silver). This is God's word and His prophecy. These are God's plans governed by His divine providential authority. Judas did exactly what God predestined him in the Scriptures to do. But it was not God that betrayed Christ. Judas did! Speaking of the veracity and certainty of the Word, Jesus declared, "the Scriptures cannot be broken" (John 10:35). God controls everything but He does not do everything, yet everything is under His authority. In Rev. 17:17, it states, "For God has put it into their hearts to fulfill His purpose, to be of one mind, and to give their kingdom to the beast, until the words of God are fulfilled" (Rev. 17:17, NKJV). Here, the passage states that "God put it in their hearts to fulfill His will," nevertheless, those kings are personally responsible for being in league with Satan and the Antichrist. They will never be able to say, "God made us give our kingdoms to the beast."

From these examples, it is clear that God who is all powerful, all knowing and fills all time and space, who *controls* all things, in whom all things are held together, does not *do* everything. Since God is sovereign everything is under His authority. There are certain things that He has committed to men, and certain things that he has committed unto angels. A specific task given to angels is the tactical restraint of demonic forces, and this makes sense because both holy angels and fallen angels / demons are of the same ontological order.

There are some well-documented cases of this in both Old and New Testaments. One of the most graphic accounts of an angelic and demonic tactical conflict is found in Daniel chapter 10. In this text, Daniel had prayed a prayer of intersession on the behalf of Israel, in response an angel was dispatched to Daniel with the answer, but the angel had a confrontation with the demonic ruler of the Kingdom of Persia. Let's take a look at the passage beginning at verse 4:

> On the twenty-fourth day of the first month, while I was by the bank of the great river, that is, the Tigris, I lifted my eyes and looked, and behold, there was a certain **man** dressed in linen, whose waist was girded with *a belt of* pure gold of Uphaz. **His** body also *was* like beryl, **his** face had the appearance of lightning, **his** eyes were like flaming torches, **his** arms and feet like the gleam of polished bronze, and the sound of **his** words like the sound of a tumult. Now I, Daniel, alone saw the vision, while the men who were with me did not see the vision; nevertheless, a great dread fell on them, and they ran away to hide themselves. So I was left alone and saw this great vision; yet no strength was left in me, for my natural color turned to a deathly pallor, and I retained no strength. But I heard the sound of **his** words; and as soon as I heard the sound of **his** words, I fell into a deep sleep on my face, with my face to the ground. Then behold, a hand touched me and set me trembling on my hands and knees. **He** said to me, "O Daniel, man of high esteem, understand the words that I am about to tell you and stand upright, for I have now been sent to you." And when **he** had spoken this word to me, I stood up trembling. Then **he** said to me, "Do not be afraid, Daniel, for from the first day that you set

your heart on understanding *this* and on humbling yourself before your God, your words were heard, and I have come in response to your words. "But the prince of the kingdom of Persia was withstanding me for twenty-one days; then behold, Michael, one of the chief princes, came to help me, for I had been left there with the kings of Persia. "Now I have come to give you an understanding of what will happen to your people in the latter days, for the vision pertains to the days yet *future*."

Daniel 10:4-14

The passage describes an angelic being whose body had the appearance of beryl (a beautiful crystal like stone) and a face that looked like lightning. When Daniel saw this angel, he was so traumatized that he fainted (vs. 6-11) and the men that were with him couldn't see the angel but felt his presence and fled for their lives. This is absolutely mind-boggling. This angel was delayed three weeks by the demonic principality who ruled over the kingdom of Persia. Amazingly, this angel needed backup from Michael the archangel. These angelic wars are serious! It is also interesting that this angel was referred to one time as a "man," seven times as "his" and three times as "he." All these are masculine pronouns, a fact that is also relevant to the 2 Thessalonians 2 texts where masculine pronouns are also used.

At the close of Daniel 10, the angel makes an astounding statement. Beginning at verse 20, the angel says:

> However, I will tell you what is inscribed in the writing of truth. Yet there is no one who stands firmly with me against these *forces* except Michael your prince.

Daniel 10:21

In verse 21, the following words need no interpretation, "there is no one who stands firmly with me against these *forces* except Michael your prince." No one, except Michael, includes the Holy Spirit. The phrase *stands firmly*, comes from the Hebrew word *chazaq*[45] that means: to *bind, restrain, conquer catch, cleave, confirm, be constant, constrain.* Here we have an

---

45 Strong's Hebrew Dictionary, 2388 *stands firmly*

affirmation of responsibility to restrain these demonic principalities coming from the angel himself. As he says in the passage, "no one" restrains or withholds against these (speaking of the demonic principality of Persia) with him but Michael, who is also an angel. "No one except Michael supported Gabriel in his spiritual warfare—not because no one else was available but because no one else was needed."[46] Clearly, the Holy Spirit was not the tactical agent of restraint here that detained this demonic principality neither was He needed. Remember, everything is under God's authority and control, but He does not do everything.

The reason I chose to use an Old Testament example of tactical angelic restraint of demonic forces, is because pretribulationist normally refer to the Old Testament passages to demonstrate the restraining ministry of the Holy Spirit. Two of the main passages are Genesis 6:3, and Isaiah 59:19b. The pretribulationist are stuck here because they cannot retreat to a "the restraining ministry of the Holy Spirit is a New Testament, Church age phenomena," while at the same time having to default to Old Testament passages to prove the same point. They simply cannot have it both ways. Therefore, the restraining ministry concept promoted by pre-trib based on the 2 Thessalonians 2 text, is largely a conceptual theological conclusion based on answering the question, *who else can it be*, then "supposedly" eliminating all other possibilities then defaulting to the Holy Spirit.

Ironically, if one was to apply the strict dispensational interpretation to Isaiah 59:19, then this passage cannot be used to prove a Holy Spirit restraining ministry in the Church age anyway, because this passage deals with God delivering Jacob or Israel. Remember, it is the pretribulationist's argument that says the tribulation is the time of Jacob's trouble and therefore does not apply to the church, so then you cannot have it both ways and use Isaiah 59:19b, which is clearly talking about Jacob (see verse 20).

Our next example of tactical restraint is found in Revelation 12, where Satan and one-third of the angels are ousted from heaven. The text reads:

And there was war in heaven. Michael and his angels fought

---

46 New American Commentary, Volume 18, pg. 288, Daniel

against the dragon, and the dragon and his angels fought back. But he was not strong enough, and they lost their place in heaven. The great dragon was hurled down—that ancient serpent called the devil, or Satan, who leads the whole world astray. He was hurled to the earth, and his angels with him.

Rev. 12:7-9, NIV

This text is another very clear example of tactical restraint of angelic or demonic forces. For this verse I chose to use the NIV because it expresses the fact that Satan *was not strong enough* for Michael and his angels. Again, Michael was obviously acting under the providential and judicial authority of God, but the tactical agents of restraint were the angels which demonstrates our theme that God controls everything, but He does not do everything.

THREE REASONS FOR THE MASCULINE AND NEUTER PRONOUN

As it relates to the 2 Thessalonians 2 text there are three reasons why the use of the masculine and neuter pronouns are appropriate.

1) We do not know the names of the holy angels except for Michael, Gabriel, Lucifer or Satan, and Apollyon (a fallen angel). An explanation for this can be found in Judges chapter 13, beginning at verse 17 which says: "And Manoah said unto the angel of the lord, What is thy name, that when thy sayings come to pass we may do thee honor? And the angel of the Lord said unto him, why askest thou thus after my name seeing it is a *secret*" (Judges 13:17-18, KJV). The NIV translates it, He replied, "Why do you ask my name? It is beyond *understanding*." God obviously didn't feel it was necessary to reveal angelic names to us because as the NIV puts it: their names are, "beyond understanding" and beyond our intellectual ability to articulate or even comprehend (ref. Judges 13:18, NIV).

2) Since angels are referred to in the masculine gender (man, he, his, etc.), Paul's use of the pronoun "he" is consistent with how angels are referred to throughout the Bible. And, since he had already told the Thessalonians in a former visit who the restrainer was, Paul's lack of specificity by only using "he" is appropriate.

3) The use of the neuter word "what" is appropriate as well because the abyss is a *place*, not a *person*. Remember the bottomless pit is under lock and key, and it is an angelic duty to open and close it. The holy angels operating under the providential authority of the Lord, are the tactical agents who bind demons with chains and cast them into this pit. The beast cannot ascend out of the bottomless pit on his own accord. He must be loosed by the holy angel(s), who are responsible for restraining demons, and locking and unlocking the Abyss. Though Paul does not say anything about an angel or the abyss in 2 Thes. 2, he doesn't have to because Revelation fills in those blanks for us. Besides, John was not the only one caught up into heaven to receive revelations, Paul was as well (2 Cor. 12:1-4).

When you factor in all of the afore stated, it becomes clear how the mis-interpretation of these two words, "he," and "what," has affected how Christians view end-time events. Whole doctrines have been spun off of the interpretation of these words. People are taught that the Holy Spirit will be taken from the earth before Daniel's 70th week arrives, when there are no scriptures that state that! This is a theological conclusion without any explicit scriptures to back that up.

Remember, Paul didn't say who the "he" was. The Holy Spirit restrainer was pretrib's "who else can it be" default option, after supposedly eliminating all the other options. But this position (i.e. Walvoord, Pentecost and others) did not consider angels, let alone ruling them out, which makes their conclusions based on an incomplete examination of all biblical possibilities. On this point I wrote to both of these scholars, which neither one of them had a good answer (more on this later). Explicit accounts of angelic restraint are found in the Bible; therefore, it is no excuse for not including them in their examination, particularly since we know the beast ascends from the Abyss. Neither can it be overlooked that there are explicit scriptural references that show evil angels restrained or bound with chains (2 Peter 2:4, Jude 1:6, Rev. 9:13-14, Rev. 20:1-3).

According to pretrib, the removal of the Holy Spirit is one of two things (the apostasy and the revealing) that must occur prior to the revealing of the Antichrist. The Church must be caught up (via the rapture), when the Holy Spirit departs. Since the Holy Spirit is to be taken prior to the revealing of the Antichrist, who is to be revealed to the world at the signing of the seven-year peace treaty in Israel, which starts Daniel's 70th week, then the Church must be raptured prior to the 70th week of Daniel. Since all of Daniel's seventieth week is considered by pretrib to be the wrath of God, (a point to which I disagree), the Church must be raptured prior to Daniel's 70th week.

All the teaching that declares that the Church will be gone before the revealing of the Antichrist causes Christians to interpret the book of Revelation as being mostly informational. The pretribulationists insists the church is not even mentioned in Revelation between chapters 4 through 19 which to them, backs their theory that the Church has already been raptured. Consequently, since sixteen chapters of Revelation do not apply to the Church, many do not bother to read, or teach, apply or take heed to the message that God intended for the Church. The real tragedy is that God has given the Church valuable information about the last generation of Church saints, but the Church cannot benefit from the message they have been trained to ignore.

Just as Jesus charged the scholars of His day, that controlled the interpretation and application of the scriptures, "...Thus have ye made the commandment of God of none effect by your tradition" (Mt 15:6), so modern-day scholars do the same. Just for the sake of argument, what if pretrib is wrong, what's at stake? What if the Church is still here while Antichrist is here? What if all the forewarning of the prophetic scriptures, found in Revelation, were meant for the Church? How would those Christians who find themselves present during the time of Antichrist, respond to having no access to the economic system, coupled with the threat of imprisonment and death? How would they stand during such times? Would the saints under these circumstances suffer any worse than what Jesus, the apostles, the Christians of the first three centuries, and all the martyrs down through the centuries, and even today suffered? Here is what the Bible says:

> ...There were others who were tortured, refusing to be released so that they might gain an even better resurrection. Some faced jeers and flogging, and even chains and imprisonment. They were put to death by stoning; they were sawed in two; they were killed by the sword. They went about in sheep-

skins and goatskins, destitute, persecuted, and mistreated—the world was not worthy of them. They wandered in deserts and mountains, living in caves and in holes in the ground. Hebrews 11:35-38, NIV

After reading that passage and considering all the suffering for Jesus' sake that believers and Christians have endured for centuries, is it reasonable to believe that 21st century Christians are somehow beyond going through the same thing? Who in God's name do we think we are?

8

The Correspondence with Pentecost and Walvoord

On May 9, 1997, I wrote a letter to Dwight Pentecost requesting that he review the paper I wrote exposing a major flaw in the pretrib theory. Below is an excerpt of the letter. The full document can be reviewed in the Appendix.

> Dr. Pentecost I humbly request that you render an objective opinion of the position which I espouse. Please, by all means be critical. Since I use your text as a basis for some of my arguments, I feel it is appropriate that you respond to my arguments. By no means am I critical of you as a renown theologian with a worldwide reputation. But my main concern is with the church at large, and what could happen if in fact current dispensational theories were incorrect.

> You should know that I did send Dr. Walvoord a version of this paper back in the summer of 1996 while I was living in the Dallas area. Though Dr. Walvoord disagreed with my position, he didn't really say why, nor did he refute what I had said. Therefore, that could almost be interpreted as acquiescing. To avoid this, I have included some questions at the end of the paper to be answered, and I also invite your commentary.

> Dr. Pentecost, I know you're a busy man. And I am not a renowned theologian like you. I also realize that I don't carry enough academic status for you to take time to respond to. But as a fellow minister of the gospel, I humbly ask you to please do so. I believe in sound doctrine, and if I'm in error, then show me that I may accurately glorify our Lord and Savior Jesus Christ to the best of my ability.

The tone of this letter is clear. My concern was for the church at large. I was not looking to score some "I gotcha points." The purpose of writing to these scholars was to have them critique the points and objections that I raise that challenges the validity of certain aspects of their doctrine. The particular point I chose to challenge them on was their failure to recognize the restraining ministry of angels. This was not a refutation of the whole position. In my paper (see appendix) I clearly demonstrated that angels are used as agents of restraint. I used scriptural texts from both Old and New Testaments. Secondly, I demonstrated from the scriptures that there is a demonic aspect of the beast that is restrained and imprisoned in the bottomless pit. This demonic principality can only be active in the Antichrist after being loosed from his restraints and set free from the confines of the abyss.

I clearly pointed out that the chief principality and power of all evil, Satan himself, was restrained, imprisoned in the bottomless pit, and rendered powerless by a single unnamed angel. In the closing of my paper, I make the following statement:

"It should be noted that what I've developed here is not a complete argument. I intentionally only focused in on certain aspects of my argument to open up a dialog and pose some questions. I clearly understand pretrib theory is not solely based on just Second Thessalonians. My Holy Spirit restrainer argument only opens the can of worms, and trust me, without that pretrib 2 Thessalonians 2 interpretation, there's a lot of other worms to be reckoned with. In my closing, I'm not attempting to eisogete the ideas of my paper into the 2 Thes. 2 text. I'm simply saying, in the absence of identifying information in 2 Thessalonians 2, why wouldn't we use relevant, explicit eschatological passages that directly answer these questions in a biblically pragmatic way? Note: please answer these questions, considering all that I have put forth in this paper."[47]

47 Appendix, paper written by Dennis J. Woods, sent to J. Dwight Pentecost at Dallas Theological Seminary on 5-9-1997, pg 107-119.

DR. J. DWIGHT PENTECOST

The following are Dr. Pentecost's answers to three questions I posed to him in the paper:

Question 1: Why have theorist opted for implicit scriptures to identify the restrainer when there are explicit eschatological passages that deal directly with his identity? And why have these passages been overlooked?[48]

Pentecost's Answer: Whereas Pentecost responded to the next two questions, he skipped this one. I suspect it is because the biblical arguments that I provided cannot be refuted. The information about the angel that bound Satan and threw him in the abyss; the same abyss from where the beast ascends, is explicitly stated in Revelation. However, pretrib theorists never used this information when they developed their theories. By leaving the restraining angel / bottomless pit dynamic out, they failed to examine thoroughly all biblical options—though they claim they have. Dr. Pentecost didn't answer this question because there is no good answer as to why pretribulationist didn't use passages in Revelation that speak directly to the restrainer issue. The fact that he was silent on this critical issue speaks volumes.

Question 2: Why can't angels be the restrainers?

Pentecost's Answer: "they can be agents but only under authority, you make them independent."[49]

I was very surprised that Dr. Pentecost, in his own handwriting on my paper, and in his return letter he sent to me, admitted that angels indeed are agents of restraint.[50] That means this esteemed theologian just contradicted everything he had written on this subject. If he knew that, why then were not angels included as an option in his restrainer theory? By not including angels means simultaneously that he excluded angels. This also means that he did not include an obvious biblical restrainer option, when he knew that it existed. He knew it but said nothing. That alone is a serious indictment.

Angels are not some obscure reference dug up from some obscure piece

48 See Appendix, Dennis Woods paper pg 119 question 1
49 Ibid 119, question 2
50 Pentecost letter, pg 120

of ancient literature. Angels, in whom Satan is one, are very prominent throughout apocalyptic literature and elsewhere in the Bible. How could anyone miss angels unless they didn't want to see them? And when he makes the statement "they can be agents but only under authority," it's a moot point because there is nothing in existence outside of God's authority anyway.

Secondly, Dr. Pentecost then makes a claim that I *do not* make in my paper, that my angelic restrainer argument destroys pretrib theory. I clearly state that I realize pretrib "is not" solely based on this alone.[51] However, by arguing against a point that I do not make, indicates that he understood the problem this causes for the pretrib rapture theory based on the 2 Thes. 2 text. He is fully aware that if there is another viable biblical candidate for the restrainer, it undercuts all that he and other dispensational authors have written and taught concerning this matter.

Dr. Pentecost also claims that I made angels "independent."[52] Elsewhere in his return letter to me, he said that I make angels "sovereign." Besides certain references to the *Angel of the Lord* which usually designates a manifestation of the Logos[53] assuming an angelic form, I have never heard of a sovereign angel. Angel means *messenger* and by implication means one sent with a message which is a functionary role. I never heard of a *sovereign* functionary. There was nothing in my paper or in any of my teachings, where I remotely suggest the sovereignty of angels. Dr. Pentecost's response was surprisingly baseless, but it was the best one he had, because you can't argue with the restraining angel of Rev. 20:1-4.

In the appendix of this book is the entire paper, (grammatical imperfections and all), and I'll let you be the judge of whether I make angels "independent or sovereign." It is flattering to know that a baseless rebuttal was the best point that this esteemed theologian could muster up to counter my angelic restrainer argument.

In his letter to me dated May 20, 1997, and on my paper,[54] Dr. Pentecost responds, "Even though they may be agents in restraint it is still God (the Holy Spirit) who actually restrains." I found this statement to be very

---

51 See Appendix, Dennis Woods paper pg 118
52 Ibid pg 119, question 2
53 Pulpit Commentary, – Zechariah,
54 Pentecost letter, pg 120

interesting. Since Dr. Pentecost used the words *actually restrains*, then he must be aware of some explicit text that *actually* verifies that assertion. You see, if there were a passage of Scripture that did show the Holy Spirit in the act of restraining Satan or the Antichrist, then there would not have been a controversy in the first place. No one would have had to ask who is the restrainer. The case would be settled. However, when Dr. Pentecost asserts it's the Holy Spirit that *actually restrains*, where is that text in the Bible that shows the Holy Spirit restraining angelic principalities? The beast that ascends out of the bottomless pit is a demonic principality. Once again, we end up with their assertion that cannot be backed with Scripture—that's the problem with aspects of pretribulationism. A theologian declares, "this is how it has to be," not the Bible.

However, there are several passages where angels *actually* restrain. Dr. Pentecost would have been better off saying the Holy Spirit providentially or judiciously authorizes restraint, but the angels *actually do* the restraining. Remember, we're not talking about the Spirit restraining Satan's activity against humans. Indeed, the Holy Spirit *is our helper not the angel's helper* (see chapter 9). For example, in Revelation 20:1-3, if the passage said, "And I saw the Holy Spirit" or even "the Spirit" come down from heaven, having the key of the bottomless pit and a great chain…," then what Pentecost asserts would be irrefutable. But who *actually* comes down from heaven with the key to the bottomless pit, and has a chain in his hand, lays hold on Satan, binds him, sets a seal on him, throws him in the abyss and locks it—is an angel. Granted, the Spirit may have ordered this, but He certainly was not the one who *actually* restrained the devil. Yes, God providentially controls everything, but He does not do everything.

Question 3: Since the scriptures tell us that the beast ascends out of the abyss, why can't the abyss be what's holding the beast back/down?

Pentecost's Answer: Once again, Dr. Pentecost does not answer the key aspect of this question directly.[55] I suspect, because the biblical information itself cannot be refuted and it would argue against their theory. Whenever a statement cannot be refuted, silence is the best answer. However, he did circle the word beast and then questions: "is this Satan

---

55 Appendix pg 119, question 3

or the Antichrist?" I couldn't believe my eyes. To avoid dealing with the fact that the beast ascends out of the bottomless pit (Rev. 17:8), to confuse the issue on what is explicit in Scripture, Dr. Pentecost asks, "is this Satan or Antichrist?"[56] That is ridiculous because he knows it cannot be Satan. Satan is not cast into the bottomless pit until the beginning of the Millennium (Rev. 20:1-3) and stays there for a thousand years. We all know that the Devil is the prince and the power of the air, and the god of this present age (Eph. 2:2, 2 Cor. 4:4) and not in the abyss.

Other commentators, including John MacArthur, another pretrib theorist, understand that the beast that is released from the bottomless pit is a demonic principality and not Satan (MacArthur Bible Commentary, pg 2028). In Rev. 12:9-12, Satan is casted out of "heaven" to the earth. If Satan were in the bottomless pit, he would be inactive and powerless, (Rev. 20:3) which has not been the case since the fall of Adam. However, in any case, this question doesn't mitigate my argument at all. The fact is whether Satan or the beast, if they were in the bottomless pit, they were locked in by angels, and the bottomless pit itself was the prison that kept them in place. God made the abyss to be impregnable and escape proof.

Elsewhere, in my paper Dr. Pentecost suggests that the angel of Rev. 20:1-3, is Christ. To avoid conceding to the point I made, he makes another outrageous claim that is even more problematic. By saying "this refers to Christ,"[57] Dr. Pentecost has introduced another candidate for the restrainer. Now, Jesus is the restrainer? Dr. Pentecost does not make that claim in any of his other works where he suggests that the resurrected Lord of Glory leaves His exalted throne to restrain Satan, an angelic being that He created. This is a preposterous response. I'm glad that I preserved his letter and my paper to prove that these were his actual responses to me. Without proof, no one would ever believe that the late great Dr. J. Dwight Pentecost made such a baseless statement—but he did.

The restraint of demonic beings is a delegated angelic responsibility. Since the beast ascends from the abyss (a prison), tactical restraint must be part of the equation. Failing to factor this in leads to incorrect conclusions. Just as a judge may order a criminal to be jailed, the judge would not be expected to personally take the prisoner and lock him up and

56 Ibid, pg 119
57 Ibid, pg 110

guard him. If we as men, would not expect that of a mere human judge, how is it that we would expect this of God the eternal sovereign judge. On pages 107-110 is the section of the paper where I methodically dismantle Pentecost's arguments based on his reference work, *Things To Come*. I use his assertions against him. What's remarkable is his lack of response. He makes no substantive counterpoints when I attack his work directly. Pentecost's rebuttals are based on a sovereignty of angels premise. However, that is a point that I do not make.

Next, Dr. Pentecost makes this statement.

"You seem to feel that in establishing angels as the restrainers you have destroyed pretribulationism. This is a fallacy. You have attacked only one of the bases for the position."[58]

Once again, it is important to notice what Dr. Pentecost doesn't make comments on. He doesn't comment or counter on my point about the beast ascending out of the bottomless pit. He doesn't comment on the fact that the bottomless pit is secured by angels. He doesn't comment on the angel that literally restrains Satan and throws him in the abyss. He doesn't comment on the fact that angels are referred to in the masculine gender, and the *what* that *withholds* is a place, i.e., the Abyss, not a person requiring a neuter reference. He doesn't say that I am wrong about the angels at all. He doesn't attack the *substance* of my argument, but what he attacks is the *impact* of my argument on pretrib.

What he does attack is a point that I do not make. I clearly say that pretrib is not solely based on the Holy Spirit restrainer. Furthermore, I believe he clearly understood that if the Holy Spirit is not the restrainer of 2 Thes. 2, then you cannot use that passage to teach that the Church is removed before the revealing of the Antichrist. Pentecost is defending against the impact that he realizes not having the Holy Spirit as the restrainer has on a pretrib rapture theory. Other than that, he had no substantive responses, nor did he overcome my arguments. In essence what he is saying is, "okay you're right about the angels. So what. It's only one part of the position anyway." My response, I'm not right. The Bible is right. Pretribulationist are the ones who didn't consult the

---

58 Dwight Pentecost letter, 5-20-1997, pg 120

Scriptures. My paper is titled *The Holy Angels, God's Ministers of Restraint.* I wasn't addressing any other aspect of pretrib. The problem is if there is a gaping hole in a major premise, there will be other breaches in that doctrinal structure.

However, what I find most interesting is how Dr. Pentecost ended his letter. "I consider that I have said all I intend to say on your view and do not expect to carry on further discussion about it."[59] This was rather blunt considering my letter to him where I state, "...my main concern is with the church at large, and what could happen if in fact dispensational theories are incorrect."[60] If Mid-trib, Post-trib, and the version of Pre-wrath position I teach (which is different than Rosenthal) are wrong, and pretrib is correct, there is no harm done because the rapture would occur sooner than those positions expect. But if pretrib is wrong, what's at stake? Millions of Christians worldwide that expected a pretrib rapture, would be caught flatfooted by times they were promised they would miss. This is the question most pretribers do not have the courage to ask. "What happens if we got this wrong?"

However, judging by the tone of Dr. Pentecost's response, he wasn't concerned about that, he was more concerned about protecting the institution and tradition of pretribulationism. I also believe that he took issue with me for nailing him on the points he makes about the restrainer using his own material. By ending his letter the way he did, he must have felt he was sweeping my challenge under the rug. However, the truth cannot be swept away. Now it's available for everyone to see.

DR. JOHN WALVOORD

In regards to the late great Dr. John Walvoord, I also sent him the same paper. The following is part of his response letter to me:

> "You do not seem to realize that this is only a small portion of the pretribulational position, and you do not answer the many other indications that the rapture is before the tribulation."[61]

What Dr. Walvoord is referring to is the main premise of my paper that

59 Ibid, pg 120
60 Dennis Woods letter to Pentecost, pg 106
61 Appedix, Walvoord letter pg 121

calls pretrib out on the fact that they did not include all the possible options for determining who the restrainer of 2 Thes. 2, could be. However, I find it interesting that in view of the irrefutable evidence I present from Rev. 17 and 20, showing the relationship between the restraining angel, the bottomless pit, and the beast that ascends from the pit, he shifts to a "you don't seem to realize this (the interpretation that the restrainer is the Holy Spirit) is only a small portion of the pretrib position...." Now that I have called out scholars as himself on missing an obvious biblical restrainer directly related to the beast, Walvoord attempts to marginalize the importance of the concept of the Holy Spirit restrainer to the pretrib theory, by stating "this is only a small portion of the pretribulational position."

Additionally, it is important to note what Walvoord *does not* say, "you have ineffectively attacked this portion of the pretribulational position." Nor does Walvoord say, "you have incorrectly asserted that angels are restrainers." In effect, what Walvoord response means is that I *have* decisively countered the Holy Spirit restrainer aspect, but as Dr. Walvoord rebuts, "this is only a small part of the position." He follows that remark with, "and you do not answer the many other indications that the rapture is before the tribulation." However, the focus of this paper was not about the other aspects of pretrib. My paper exposes what pretrib has neglected from the Scriptures concerning the restraint of the Antichrist. My thesis is that the beast ascends out of a locked prison called the abyss, in which holy angel(s) literally do the restraining. In his response to me, none of this does Dr. Walvoord address or counter. The question is why didn't he? The simple answer is you cannot argue with the Scriptures. I successfully point out what they neglected to include.

However, to the point Dr. Walvoord makes, it's true, 2 Thes. 2 is only one of several *passages* used to support pretrib, but it is in no way "small." In fact, it is a *major* part of the position. Pretribulationists consider the removal of the Holy Spirit, as a "reversal of Pentecost" (see *Things to Come* pg. 262). That's not small, that's monumental, and fundamental to their position. And what's this so-called reversal of Pentecost based? Identifying the "he" of 2 Thes. 2:6-7, as the Holy Spirit who is supposed to be removed in the same way as He came.

According to pretrib, before the Antichrist is revealed, the Holy Spirit is taken out of the way and all the Christians, dead and alive, leave too in the rapture. As a result of this removal, all the works of the Spirit such as, infilling, baptizing into the body of Christ, sealing, transforming and empowering, anointing for service and so on, all cease as well. Therefore, this is not some "small portion" of their doctrine—it is a pillar! Now that I have effectively countered the Holy Spirit argument, Walvoord wants to downplay the significance pretrib places on the Holy Spirit restrainer position. Not a chance!

In *Things to Come*, Walvoord also chimes in when he states,

> There is little evidence that believers will be indwelt by the Spirit during the tribulation. . . . The tribulation period . . . seems to revert back to Old Testament conditions in several ways; and in the Old Testament period, saints were never permanently indwelt except in isolated instances, though a number of instances of the filling of the Spirit and of empowering for service are found. Taking all the factors into consideration, there is no evidence for the indwelling presence of the Holy Spirit in believers in the tribulation.[62]

Let's unpack what is being stated here. Walvoord is saying the so-called tribulation saints are not indwelt by the Holy Spirit. Why is this stated? Because pretrib teaches that the Holy Spirit is the restrainer that is removed by this point. Since that is the case, it follows that the so-called tribulation saints cannot be a part of the Church, because they do not have the Holy Spirit who baptizes believers into the body of Christ, which is the Church, and seals them to the day of redemption. However, none of this is true if the Holy Spirit was not who Paul was speaking of in 2 Thes. 2:6-7. Without the Holy Spirit being the restrainer, there is no basis to claim that the tribulation saints do not have the Holy Spirit. Neither is there a basis to claim that they are not a part of the Church. This is not some small part of pretribulationism. This is major.

In his book *The Rapture Question*, speaking of the Holy Spirit restrainer factor Dr. Walvoord also asserts,

> If, therefore, the restrainer of 2 Thessalonians 2 be identified

---
62 *Things To Come*, pg 263

as the Holy Spirit, another evidence is produced to indicate the translation of the church before the final tribulation period will begin on earth. While in the realm of debatable conclusions if left unsupported by other scriptural evidence, it constitutes a confirmation of the teaching that the church will be translated before the Tribulation.[63]

Does what Dr. Walvoord say in his rebuttal to me, square with this statement? Does it sound like Walvoord is treating this like a "small portion?" No, as a matter of fact, he states if left unsupported by other scriptural evidence, *this passage constitutes a confirmation....*" Too late to back-peddle here! Identifying the Holy Spirit as being the restrainer of 2 Thes. 2:6-7, is fundamental to the concept of a pretrib rapture. No one is asserting that pretrib is solely based on this. Walvoord and Pentecost are forced to retreat to that argument, because what I have presented about the beast ascending from the abyss and the restraining angel, completely undercuts their Holy Spirit restrainer argument, and they know it.

In the second paragraph of his letter to me Dr. Walvoord writes "Obviously you have not examined correctly what it means for the Holy Spirit to be removed as stated in 2 Thessalonians 2."[64] First of all, the "text" does not state that the "Holy Spirit" is removed, because Paul doesn't identify who the restrainer is. You cannot say it is the Holy Spirit when the text does not state it as such. What that amounts to is a typical pretribulationist interpolation. Dr. Walvoord is taking a definitive position based on an unsubstantiated interpretation that is not explicitly stated in that text. The stance he and others take is, "we say it's the Holy Spirit and that's the end of the matter." Many of these scholars are arrogant and take the position of, "we write the reference books. We teach in the seminaries, we are respected, therefore, our word is final." However, I beg to differ. The Scriptures trump everyone's opinion and everyone's degree.

In the next sentence he admits that "the text is not entirely clear," although he doesn't treat it that way in the books that he has written, where he emphatically states that the Holy Spirit is to be removed. What's interesting Dr. Walvoord does not address any of the material that I provide which proves angels are agents of restraint. He sidesteps

63 *The Rapture Question*, John Walvoord, pg 82
64 Appendix, Walvoord letter pg 121

that altogether by saying "I cannot follow your arguments nor conclusions." What's there not to follow Dr. Walvoord?

If Dr. Walvoord could have dismantled my argument, he would have, because it is more effective to attack the major premises of an argument, not the implications. The fact that angels are involved in the restraint of demonic spirits detained in the abyss, cannot be refuted because it is biblically explicit. But like Dr. Pentecost, none of Dr. Walvoord's work considers or excludes angels, a point that Dr. Pentecost concedes in his response to me, when he admits, "angels can be restrainers." Nor does he address the fact that the beast is also a demonic principality who ascends out of the bottomless pit. He skips over all these points and retreats to the timing of the rapture response, which my paper does not specifically address.

I believe the reason he responds this way is because he knows my assertions would impact the timing of the rapture, moving it away from it occurring before the man of sin is revealed. The only way this aspect of the pretrib theory works, is you must have the Holy Spirit being the restrainer that is to be "taken out of the way."

Dr. Walvoord says: "...and the earlier portion of 2 Thessalonians 2 that clearly places the rapture before the revelation of the man of sin..."[65] Again, this text does not *clearly* place the rapture as being prior to the revealing of the Antichrist. First off, the only way that interpretation works is if you accept the premise that the restrainer "to be taken out of the way" is the Holy Spirit. Because without the Holy Spirit being the restrainer of 2 Thes. 2:6-7, you don't have a translation of the saints or the removal of the Spirit in these verses. If there is another biblical restrainer, then you cannot use 2 Thes. 2 text as proof for a pretribulational rapture.

Dr. Walvoord then ends the letter with this statement: "No doubt none of us are entirely correct in all of our understanding...."[66] I'm glad that he says none of us is entirely correct; hopefully he realized that pretrib theorists did not examine all biblical options for the restrainer. The fact that I'm right about angels perhaps was too much for him to concede di-

---

65 Appendix, Walvoord letter, pg 121, para. 2
66 Ibid

rectly. Again, this was a point that Dr. Pentecost at least conceded—"angels are restrainers."[67]

Pretrib theorist typically teach the pretrib rapture theory as if it were *not a theory*, they teach it as a foregone conclusion. As a matter of fact, the word "theory" is no longer associated with this doctrine at all. In Dr. Pentecost's book *Things To Come*, you will find these words The Pretribulation Rapture "Theory" (ref. *Things To Come*, chapter 8, pg. 193). However, look at more recent Pretribulation works, and you won't find the word theory associated with this doctrine any longer. They stopped calling it a theory intentionally. A theory is a supposition. A *supposition*, is an *uncertain* or *unproven* belief. However, they don't want to tell people they are not sure. These scholars would rather build hope on a theory, instead of being honest and saying we are not sure.

In the closing of his letter, Dr. Walvoord makes an interesting comment, "No doubt, none of us are entirely correct in all of our understanding, but I cannot follow your arguments or your conclusions."[68] That's funny, Dr. Pentecost clearly understood what I was saying and so did D.A. Carson.

THE THESSALONIAN EPISTLES COME BEFORE REVELATION ARGUMENT

Finally, a last point that I would like to make is some will argue is that Paul could not have been referring to the information written in Revelation, when he wrote Second Thessalonians, because Revelation was not written until decades later. Though it is true that the book of Revelation was not written in Paul's day, the date it was written is not the issue at hand. The issue is that the information comprising both 2 Thessalonians 2 and Revelation comes from the same source. Both are divine revelations. Paul emphatically speaks of him receiving his doctrines by way of revelation and that he was not taught them by man, but by Christ (Gal. 1:12).

Paul goes further to explain about being caught up into the third heaven or paradise. Though it was not distinguishable whether he was in the body or apart from the body (probably the latter see Rev. 1:10, 4:1-2). Paul said he "was caught up to paradise and heard inexpressible things

67 Appendix, pg. 119, question 2
68 Appendix Walvoord letter, pg. 121

that no one is permitted to tell" (2 Corinthians 12:4, NIV). Paul obviously heard things he could and things he could not repeat (see Rev. 10:4). This explains how Paul could have known the same things John would later write about in Revelation, without Paul needing to rely on John's writings or vice versa, because their revelations came from the same source— heaven and the Lord. This is why John wrote about the same things as did Daniel, who lived hundreds of years before John wrote Revelation.

9
NOT EVEN MICHAEL?

All doctrines and traditions evolve over time. The Calvinism we have today has expanded beyond what Calvin actually taught during his life. The same is true with those who followed Martin Luther in what became known as the *Protestant Reformation*. As more is learned and discovered, doctrines are fine-tuned and revised. The same is true for pretribulationism. One area of revision is considering angels for the restrainer. Though Walvoord, Pentecost and many of the other pillars of dispensationalism did not include angels as a possibility for the restrainer of 2 Thessalonians 2, others have.

As stated earlier, in the *Theological Dictionary of the New Testament*, vol.2, pg. 828-829, the article on the restrainer (*katecho*) suggests that the restrainer "might be an angel." Also, in the NIV Zondervan Study Bible, the note on Who is the Restrainer" list historic options for the restrainer, he then offers Michael as a possibility. The following is a summation of the *NIV Zondervan Study Bible's* comments.

> The last proposal, though not widely held, is strongly support-
> ed by allusions to Daniel 10-12. Michael the archangel referred
> to in the text as "one of the chief princes" is said to withstand
> or restrain the evil angels (demonic principality over Persia, see
> Daniel 10:13, 20-21). Since Paul identifies a restraining force to
> be removed or taken out of the way in 2 Thessalonians 2, *likely*
> originated from Daniel 12:1b, where Michael and his restraining
> force is removed thereby ushering in of an unparalleled distress
> for God's people.[69]

It is suggested that it is Michael is the restrainer and that Paul in 2 Thes.

---

69 NIV Zondervan Study Bible, pg 2453, Jeffrey A.D. Weima, Who is the Restrainer?

2, was *likely* referring to Michael's role from the Daniel 10 and 12 perspective. However, it's difficult to connect those two passages. Whereas this is closer to the truth than other options, it's difficult to pin down Michael as being the angelic restrainer of second Thessalonians. Therefore, pretrib theorists have honed in on this concept and attempted to eliminate angels as restrainers altogether.

Two scholars that have written on this subject are Dr. John MacArthur and Dr. Norman Geisler. MacArthur gives his reasons why human power, ingenuity, and institutions cannot restrain Satan or the Antichrist. However, MacArthur does include one supernatural person, that being Michael the archangel, of whom he states, *Michael, does not have the power to restrain Satan* (Jude 9).[70] Similarly, speaking of the restrainer, Dr. Norman Geisler, gives his reason why Michael should be excluded by stating, *"for he could not in his own power restrain the devil."*[71] As evidenced in these examples, some have adapted and now include Michael as a restraint contender. However, MacArthur, Geisler and others still eliminate angels in general as a possible restrainer. The rationale is, if Michael cannot restrain Satan, and Michael is an archangel, then no other angel would be capable to restrain the beast or Satan either. Therefore, by eliminating Michael, the whole class of beings are also eliminated as being potential restrainers. However, as we shall see, this is patently false.

It is interesting that both MacArthur and Geisler reference the Jude 9 passage as a proof text of Michael's *inability* to restrain Satan. However, is Michael's ability or inability to stop the devil in question at all in that passage? In each case, MacArthur or Geisler gives no supportive commentary or exegesis as to why they have reached this conclusion. They just cite the proof text and then move on. The question is why? Since they use Jude 9, to back their point, let's examine that text.

> In the very same way, on the strength of their dreams these ungodly people pollute their own bodies, reject authority and heap abuse on celestial beings. But even the archangel Michael, when he was disputing with the devil about the body of Moses, did not himself dare to condemn him for slander but said, "The Lord rebuke

70 The MacArthur New Testament Commentary – 1 & 2 Thessalonians pg 277
71 Norman Geisler Systematic Theology vol. 4, pg 616

you!" Yet these people slander whatever they do not understand, and the very things they do understand by instinct—as irrational animals do—will destroy them.

Jude 8-10, NIV

This passage is very interesting. The context of Jude 9 is brought into clarity by the verse before it. Jude is clearly communicating the fallacy of the false teachers who are "ungodly *people* who pollute their own bodies and reject authority and heap abuse on celestial beings." In the NASB, the phrase "celestial beings" is translated "angelic majesties." Heaping verbal abuse on angelic majesties, even the evil ones, is something that lower human beings ought not do.

Apparently, the false teachers in focus here were doing just that. Further emphasizing their arrogance Jude writes, "Yet these people slander whatever they do not understand." This point is then emphasized by borrowing from an ancient *Pseudepigraphal*[72] book called the *Assumption of Moses*, where the account is given where Michael was disputing with the devil about the body of Moses. It says that Michael did not dare to condemn him for slander but said, "The Lord rebuke you!" The point that is being made here is that Michael was not *slanderous* toward Satan, not that he was *weaker* than Satan or that he *couldn't stop* Satan from doing what it was that he had in mind to do.

This passage has nothing to do with Michael's capability, prowess, or strength concerning his ability to confront or stop Satan. To walk away from this text with the assertion that *Michael does not have the power to restrain Satan* as MacArthur and Geisler do is totally unfounded. The fact is Satan *did not* do what he wanted to do with the body of Moses because Michael the tactical agent of restraint was there to stop him.

In 2 Peter 2:10-11, the same topic is covered but in greater detail.

> This is especially true of those who follow the corrupt desire of the flesh and despise authority. Bold and arrogant, they are not afraid to heap abuse on celestial beings; yet even angels, although they are stronger and

---

72 Pseudepigrapha means "writings falsely attributed." These are based on those books claiming OT characters as Adam, Enoch, Moses and others as their author. Some of the writings are anonymous, and not considered to be inspired.

more powerful, do not heap abuse on such beings when bringing judgment on them from the Lord. But these people blaspheme in matters they do not understand. They are like unreasoning animals, creatures of instinct, born only to be caught and destroyed, and like animals they too will perish.

2 Peter 2:10-12, NIV

Once again, we address this topic but with even more clarity. This time it is stated "yet even angels, although they are *stronger and more powerful, do not heap abuse on such beings* when bringing judgment on them from the Lord. Here the text clearly says that angels (Godly) are *stronger and more powerful* than these "celestial beings." *The Pillar Commentary* gives this insight, "Even though the (holy) angelic beings who are higher in strength and power (both honorable qualities) than they are, and thus their betters, do not bring a slanderous judgment against the "glorious ones" (i.e., fallen or evil angels)."[73] With this in mind, how is it that anyone can argue that Michael or other angels *do not have the power to restrain Satan* (MacArthur & Geisler). This text clearly indicates that Godly angels "are stronger and more powerful" than evil angels.

Certainly, you cannot make this point philosophically, but even more importantly, you cannot back up this argument with Scripture either. The whole point of both Jude and 2 Peter 2, passages have nothing to do with angelic ability, but with the fact that not even they slander or bring a railing accusation against evil angels.

Therefore, if the angels who are more powerful, don't slander celestial beings or the glorious ones, then mere humans should not do so either. Although they deserve it, Godly angels don't slander them because though evil, they are still dignitaries. A picture of this is seen when David, who had a right to kill his enemy Saul, refused to stretch out his hand against him, but referred to King Saul as the *Lord's anointed* (see 1 Sam 24:6). Though the Devil is the epitome of evil, he is still God's devil, the *anointed cherub* that covereth (Ezek. 28:14).

When going through his temptation in the wilderness, Jesus didn't slan-

---

73 The Pillar New Testament Commentary, The Letters of 2 Peter and Jude, pg 234

derously respond to Satan either. The discourse between Satan and Jesus in the wilderness was both tempered and respectful, containing no railing accusations (see Luke 4:1-21). The same is true when God and Satan conversed concerning Job's trials (Job 1:6-12).

Now that we have uncovered what Jude 9 is really about, which further exposes the weakness of their argument, we will examine two passages that directly contradict MacArthur and Geisler's assertions–that Michael or angels in general do not have the power to restrain Satan.

> Then war broke out in heaven. Michael and his angels fought against the dragon, and the dragon and his angels fought back. But he was not strong enough, and they lost their place in heaven. The great dragon was hurled down—that ancient serpent called the devil, or Satan, who leads the whole world astray. He was hurled to the earth, and his angels with him.
>
> Revelation 12:7-9, NIV

Michael and his angels kicked Satan's and his angels' butt, and then threw them out of heaven. The question is, which side does the passage say was stronger? Who are you going to believe, MacArthur, or the Scriptures? Here's another passage,

> And I saw an angel coming down out of heaven, having the key to the Abyss and holding in his hand a great chain. He seized the dragon, that ancient serpent, who is the devil, or Satan, and bound him for a thousand years. He threw him into the Abyss, and locked and sealed it over him, to keep him from deceiving the nations anymore until the thousand years were ended. After that, he must be set free for a short time.
>
> Revelation 20:1-3, NIV

This time it is not even Michael! An *unnamed angel*, singlehandedly comes down from heaven, binds (restrains) Satan, sets a containment seal over him and threw his wicked butt in the abyss. One angel, not a legion, not three, not even two, and certainly not the Holy Spirit, one angel bound

Satan by himself. Again, who are you going to believe, Geisler or the Scriptures? How could anyone expect to get away with *an angel cannot restrain Satan* argument is beyond me and is just plain wrong.

THE ABYSS, ANGEL AND ANTICHRIST CONNECTION

Walvoord, Pentecost, MacArthur, Geisler, and all the rest, fail to make the connection between the beast that comes up out of the abyss, the restraining angel that secures and does the binding, and the human dictator called the Antichrist. All these are interlinked. Though MacArthur asserts, "the Antichrist will become possessed by a great demon from the Abyss..."[74] he fails to make the necessary connection that the abyss is a locked place of detention, to which the godly angel(s) are tasked with restraining those incarcerated and secured in the abyss (Rev. 20:1-3). Geisler and others make the mistake of eliminating all angels by making a very weak case against one angel (Michael) based on the Jude 9 text.

Once again, when one digs down below the surface of these pretrib concepts and assertions, we find that they do not stand up to biblical scrutiny. Pretrib theory has many theological and conceptual tenets that are readily accepted, but cannot actually be backed by the Bible. However, its strength rest mainly on the hopes of a Church that will be raptured before any of the events of the 70th Week, or the vast majority of the events in Revelation occur. Pretrib is excellent at providing answers in a highly systematized way. The problem is most of the answers are shallow, hollow or just plain incorrect.

---

74 MacArthur Bible Commentary, pg 2028

10
THE HOLY SPIRIT IS *OUR* HELPER

In Ephesians 6, Paul gives this insight, "For our struggle is not against flesh and blood, but against the rulers, against the powers, against the world forces of this darkness, against the spiritual forces of wickedness in the heavenly places" (Eph. 6:12). Clearly, Paul is saying that our fight against evil, is not really with the people that we see, but with the real demonic power-players behind the scene. Case in point, the Antichrist, and his possession by the beast out of the bottomless pit.

Given that this is the case, God restricts what these evil angelic beings are able to do to and through humans. No human being in his own meager ability could stand up to one of these beings. It is not a fair fight at all. In comparison to them, we are nothing more than dissipating puffs of smoke or withering blades of grass. Ontologically speaking, humans are lower than angels. That being the case, when it comes to angel versus human, God sets perimeters because without them humans would completely be overwhelmed. An example of this consideration is found in 1 Cor. 10:13, where the Bible declares,

> No temptation has overtaken you except what is common to mankind. And God is faithful; he will not let you be tempted beyond what you can bear. But when you are tempted, he will also provide a way out so that you can endure it.   1 Corinthians 10:13, NIV

The question is, from where do these trials originate? Certainly, trials or test can come from God, except the evil ones. God does not send evil trials as James clearly teaches,

> Let no one say when he is tempted, "I am being tempted by God"; for God cannot be tempted by evil, and He

Himself does not tempt anyone. But each one is tempted
when he is carried away and enticed by his own lust.
James 1:13-14

From this passage, James makes it clear that evil trials and temptations
do not originate with God but are typically the outworking of people's
evil desires. However, evil temptation not only comes from evil hearts,
but from wicked spiritual entities that Paul cites in Ephesians 6. In Matthew and Luke Satan is "the tempter" (Matthew 4:3, Luke 4:13). Speaking of evil spiritual entities, God will not allow these beings to tempt
people beyond that which is common to human experience nor beyond
our limitations. In the supernatural realms there are evil enticements
that go beyond human capability to resist or withstand.

God being faithful will not allow us to be pulled into temptation beyond
what's common to humankind. In this way God's certainly restrains evil
because He knows that our warring and wrestling is not with people in
and of themselves, but is demonic in nature. Therefore, for Christians,
God gives the believer the *paraklētos*[75] the Comforter, *a one who appears in
another's behalf, mediator, intercessor, helper.* This is the Holy Spirit *our helper* (Ps.
37:40). Since humans have to fight against demonic influences, God gives
us the "helper" to resist and provide a way to escape. We must "put on all
of God's armor so that you will be able to stand firm against all strategies
of the devil" (Eph. 6:11, NLT). In the world at large, God also uses government and law enforcement as well (Rom.13:1-6).

Another way God restrains evil with humans is through angelic guards.
Psalms 34 assures, "The angel of the LORD encamps around those who
fear Him; And rescues them" (Psalm 34:7). This is what Satan ran into
with Job, an angelic barrier of sorts.

> Then Satan answered the LORD, "Does Job fear God for
> nothing? Have You not made a hedge about him and his
> house and all that he has on every side? You have blessed
> the work of his hands, and his possessions have increased
> in the land."
Job 1:9-10

When it comes to *human versus evil angels* (i.e., principalities and powers,

---

75 BDAG, A Greek-English Lexicon of the New Testament and Other Early Christian Literature, *Comforter*

rulers of the darkness, spiritual wickedness in heavenly places) God has given us *the helper*, the Holy Spirit as a way to resist, or if you will, restrain evil. However, when it comes to *holy angel* versus *evil angel*, the Holy Spirit is never mentioned as helping in these conflicts. Unambiguously, the angel told Daniel, "But I will tell you what is inscribed in the book of truth: *there is none who contends by my side against these except Michael, your prince*" (Daniel 10:21, RSV). *Keil and Delitzsch* observes, "the angel states more minutely the nature of the war which he has to carry on. He has no one who fights with him against these enemies (against the evil spirits of Persia and Greece) but Michael the angel-prince of Israel, who strongly shows himself with him, i.e., as an ally in the conflict."[76] Whether it's Dan. 10, Jude 9, Rev. 12:7-19, 20:1-3, the Holy Spirit is never found in a restraining posture in *angel versus angel* conflicts.

We cannot overlook what the angel told Daniel before commenting on Michael. The angel said, "I will tell you what is *inscribed in the book of truth.*" What exactly is this *Book of truth*, is unknown. However, what is known is that the book is not earthly nor of human origin. Albert Barnes observes,

> "They are described as written down in a book that is in the hands of God...all future events are as certain as if they were actually recorded as history, or as if they were now all written down. The angel came that he might unfold a portion of that volume and disclose the contents of its secret pages."[77]

Also speaking of the *Book of Truth*, "Mentioned nowhere else in the Scriptures. In this context, it is a book that contains the course of future events. God is truly sovereign over history.[78] The issue of the angel not receiving any help from "no one" which includes the Holy Spirit, is recorded *in the Bible* but it does not originate *from the Bible*, but finds its origin recorded in the annals of the *Book of Truth* where God's secrets for the ages are recorded in heaven. This is not a mere human's theological perspective, but this knowledge comes bearing heaven's authority in which only the heavenly host have access to its divine content. There are other books the Scriptures identify in heaven such as; the book detailing events of the believer's life (Psalm 56:8, 139:16), the *Book of Truth* (Dan.

---

76 Keil and Delitzsch Commentary on the Old Testament - Volume 9: pg 744, Ezekiel, Daniel
77 Barnes Notes on the Old Testament, Daniel 10:21
78 NIV Zondervan Study Bible, pg. 1712, Daniel 10:21

10:21), the *book of Remembrance* (Mal. 3:16), the *seven sealed scroll* (Rev. 5:1-2), the *books containing individual's works*, and the *Book of Life* (Rev. 20:12).

Finally, the Hebrews 2:16, passage seals it. "For indeed He does not give aid to angels, but He does give aid to the seed of Abraham" (NKJV). The NASB says it this way, "For assuredly He does not give help to angels...." Therefore, you never see in the Scriptures the Holy Spirit involved in angelic conflicts or God helping an angel. Why is this important? The beast that comes up from the abyss and the restraining angel constitutes an angel on angel situation. Therefore, the Holy Spirit would not be involved with this type of restraint in the first place. The Antichrist or the beast of Revelation 13, cannot start his 42 month reign until he is possessed by the beast that ascends from the bottomless pit. This is why 2 Thes. 2:6 states that Antichrist can only be revealed "in his time."

11
WHAT DIFFERENCE DOES IT MAKE?

In the final analysis, What difference does it make whether the Holy Spirit is the restrainer, or the restraint is of an angelic nature? How does that really impact modern day Christians? Well, the answer is simple. If pretrib is right and the Church is raptured before Daniel's 70th week starts, then fine, we're gone before the trouble starts. No harm done. However, if pretrib is wrong about the Holy Spirit being the one that was to be taken out of the way, along with the Church, then that would mean that millions of Christians will be caught flat-footed as the events associated with portions of Daniel's 70th week occur. Specifically, Christians would still be on earth during the time of the Antichrist, after being assured that the Church would be raptured by then.

The average Christian in America and around the world that accepts pretrib as the only viable rapture doctrine option, can hardly wrap their head around the idea of being here during the events of Daniel's 70th week, especially if it calls for dying for the faith. Historically, Christians of the first centuries and in certain countries around the world today, lived with that exact reality. Consider what John says in 1 John, "Dear children, this is the last hour; and as you have heard that the Antichrist is coming, even now many antichrists have come. This is how we know it is the last hour" (1 John 2:18, NIV). In other words, you know this is the last hour because antichrists are already present. This statement anticipates, not negates Christians seeing the Antichrist. John clearly, presupposes that the historic antichrists and the eschatological Antichrist will be a part of the Christian experience as an indicator of the "last hour."

If John had a pretrib or dispensational perspective, would it not have been more accurate to say, "as you have heard that the Antichrist is coming. However, even though there will be other antichrists to deal with as we have today, do not concern yourselves with the last Antichrist because before he comes we will already be with the Lord."

When you consider the possibility that Christians could face the eschatological Antichrist as they did historic antichrists, then the purpose of Revelation takes on a greater relevance and significance. God had a different purpose in mind for the book of Revelation, beyond being the subject of doctrinal and theological debate. Maybe God was simply revealing the end from the beginning so that the generation of Christians living during that unparalleled time in human history, would have the details and the encouragement that no matter how dark it gets, Christ and his followers win in the end.

Wouldn't it be better to teach people the whole truth? Wouldn't it be wise to reveal both sides of the coin? Is it not better to tell people what the options are, so that they could be prepared in the event the pretrib theory is wrong? Think about it, if Christians are still here, when Antichrist does come, imagine the impact it would have on them. Wouldn't it have been better to tell them what to expect in case the theories are wrong, instead of insuring that there's no possibility that they will be here? One thing that the COVID-19 pandemic taught the world is that things can change quickly for everyone on the planet within a very short time frame. It showed Christians that our churches can be shut down instantly with one executive order, and global economies can come to a screeching halt. Anger, unrest, and anarchy can ignite after one injustice and trigger global protests, social unrest, rioting and looting, turning an entire nation into a powder keg over night.

Finally, what I have covered in this book is only the beginning. In the upcoming editions of this *End-time Apologetics Series*, I will be addressing several of the principal tenets of the pretrib rapture theory. The purpose for these teachings is so Christians will be aware of the tenuous aspects of a popular doctrine that so many believers place their trust. All believers should be aware that all these eschatological doctrines are unproven theories. No one has all the answers.

As I say throughout this book, "if pretrib is correct, and we are raptured before the 70ᵗʰ Week, and everything works out *exactly* as pretrib choreographs it, then Hallelujah, we're out of here!" However, if there are problematic aspects to this theory, as I clearly demonstrate in this book that there are, that should necessitate a re-examination of that position. By doing so, Christians might be informed properly and not needlessly promote false assurance. We should not have blind loyalty to a position just for the doctrine or our alma mater, denomination, church, or our pastor's sake. Too many lives are at stake.

SEVEN RAMIFICATIONS IF THE SPIRIT IS NOT THE RESTRAINER

When I wrote Dr. Walvoord and Pentecost, it was to discuss the impact the restrainer controversy would have on Christians. I was hopeful that by exposing obvious pretrib flaws, it would start a dialog. However, Dr. Pentecost refused to discuss the matter further.[79] Dr. Pentecost also claimed, that the Holy Spirit not being the restrainer would have no impact on the pretrib rapture theory at all.[80] Since pretribulationists have determined the Spirit's removal is true, there are inevitable results that would logically follow in the wake of the Spirit's departure. However, if the Holy Spirit is not removed, then the circumstances pretrib proposes to occur to believers during that time cannot be true. In answering the question what difference does it make, the following are seven ramifications if the Spirit is not the restrainer.

1) If the Holy Spirit is not the restrainer of 2 Thes. 2:6-7, then there is no basis to insist that He is removed before the revealing of the Antichrist, whether it's in his role as the restrainer or in his redemptive work. As Dr. Walvoord stated, "this text has information found nowhere else in the Bible.[81]" Though pretrib is not solely based on this text, it's the only passage they can use to base their conjecture by drawing a direct connection between the removal of the Holy Spirit and the rapture of the Church. However, identifying the wrong restrainer sets a false expectation that Christians will be raptured before the revealing of the Antichrist.

According to pretrib, the phrase "taken out of the way" in 2 Thes. 2:7

---

79 Appendix, Pentecost Letter, pg 119
80 Appendix Pentecost marginal notes on Woods' paper, pg 108
81 The Bible Knowledge Commentary, New Testament, 2 Thessalonians chapter 2, pg 717

is in reference to the removal of the Spirit. In Joel 2:28 and Acts 2:17, God gives (pours out) the Spirit. However, there aren't any scriptures that state that God comes back "to take" or to "remove" the Spirit. Additionally, in each rapture passage, Christ always comes back for the Church. It is never said that Christ "comes back" for the Holy Spirit. Though passages such as John 14:26 inform that the Spirit was sent, however, there aren't any scriptures showing the recall of the Spirit back to heaven. That's an assertion without Biblical backing. This entire concept is totally conjectural.

2) If the Holy Spirit is not the restrainer, then the 2 Thes. 2 text cannot be used as support for a pretribulational rapture of the Church. Without the Spirit being removed here, there is no rapture of the Church in this passage at all. Secondly, the Holy Spirit is God, why would he require being "taken out of the way" or be removed? Would not the Spirit withdraw of its own volition? Who is taking authority over God the Holy Spirit, to take him out of the way? If it is the Father or the Son commanding the removal of the Spirit, where are the Scriptures to back that up? Therefore, 2 Thes. 2:6-7 cannot be used to support a pretrib rapture.

John MacArthur agrees but for a different reason. "The removal of the Holy Spirit's restraint therefore cannot be identified with the Rapture of the church, since that event takes place three and a half years earlier, before the Tribulation."[82] Where the author and MacArthur disagree is the Holy Spirit being the restrainer of that passage in the first place. Upon this basis is why I state you cannot use this passage to support a pretrib rapture particularly if the Holy Spirit is not the restrainer to whom Paul was referring. However, it should be noted that the vast majority of pretribulationists *are not* in agreement with MacArthur on not using 2 Thes. 2 text to prove a pretrib rapture. Traditionally, pretribulationists understand Antichrist's revealing occurs when the 7-year covenant is enacted (Dan. 9:27). Subsequently, they consider the entirety of Daniel's 70th week as the day of the Lord and the tribulation period.

3) If the Holy Spirit is not removed, that means all of the Spirit's salvific work and ministries to Christians and the Church continues into portions of Daniel's 70th week and the tribulation period. Pretribulationist must show explicitly that the Spirit has been removed—which they cannot.

82 MacArthur New Testament Commentary - 1 & 2 Thessalonians pg.278

THE ANTICHRIST, ANGELS & THE ABYSS

4) If the Holy Spirit is still present during the tribulation, there is no basis to teach that the *so-called* tribulation saints do not have the indwelling Holy Spirit as many pretribulationist teach.

5) If the Holy Spirit is still present during the tribulation, there is no basis for a "reversal of Pentecost" (see *Things to Come*, pg. 262). The Church began on the Day of Pentecost. A reversal of Pentecost would mean the end of the Church age. Though pretribulationists assert that the Spirit goes in the same way as he came, there aren't any Scriptures documenting a departure of the Holy Spirit as Walvoord/Pentecost and many others assert. On this point, later pretribulationists have adapted their position, because it cannot be denied that salvation is still occurring during the tribulation. Clearly, the Revelation 13 saints are Christians that remain faithful to Jesus (Rev. 14:12). Their names are written in the Lamb's book of life as implied in Rev. 13:8, 17:8. They are in the first resurrection (Rev. 20:4-6). Salvation is not possible without the regenerative work of the Holy Spirit (John 3:3-7, Rom. 8:9, 16, Eph. 1:13). No man can call Jesus Lord, especially when facing death, without the Holy Spirit, (1 Cor. 12:13).

To overcome this issue, pretrib now claims the Holy Spirit only terminates *part* of His work.[83] They claim that the Spirit is removed only in his *restrainer* role but continues His *redemptive* role. However, once again, though pretribulationist make that argument, the problem is there aren't any Scriptures that show the Spirit's splitting his functions. Also, if the Spirit leaves as *the restrainer*, but stays as *the redeemer* why should that necessitate the removal of the Church, when the church consist of the redeemed? If He's still *redeeming* that means He is also still *sealing* those whom He redeemed. The Scriptures declare, "having this seal, the Lord knows those that are his" (2 Tim. 2:19, *also see* John 6:27, 2 Cor. 1:22, Eph. 4:30, Rev. 9:4). The fact that those saved in Revelation 13:7 are called "saints" (KJV) and "God's holy people"(NIV), are undeniable proof of the Spirit's possession of these Holy ones.

6) If the Holy Spirit is not the restrainer that is to be removed, then there is no basis to claim that the saints of Revelation 13 cannot be part of the Church. The claim that the tribulation saints are a separate group only works if the Holy Spirit stops baptizing believers into the body of

83 Things to Come, pg. 263 *Baptism, indwelling, sealing, and filling, do terminate.*

Christ. If the Spirit is still here and not removed, His work in baptizing believers into the body of Christ continues. Pretribulationist may argue otherwise but they cannot prove otherwise. They must concede that people are still being saved, even during the reign of Antichrist. Revelation 14:13 states, "Then I heard a voice from heaven say, "Write this: Blessed are the dead who die in the Lord from now on." "Yes," says the Spirit, "they will rest from their labor, for their deeds will follow them."

There are two points of interest here. First these saints "die in the Lord." Paul gives the same analogy to those in Thessalonica ...the "dead in Christ" shall rise first (1 Thes. 4:16). In either case whether "in Christ" or "in the Lord," this is the Holy Spirit's work. The only way to *die in* the Lord, is to be baptized "into Christ" by the Holy Spirit. To reinforce that reality, the Spirit himself confirms this fact when He exclaims, "Yes," says the Spirit, "they will rest from their labor, for their deeds will follow them." It is appropriate for the Spirit to comment here because He is the one who places the redeemed into Christ. This is one of a few times the Spirit speaks in Revelation and righty so because it is in reference to those in whom He dwells. Therefore, Revelation refers to them as "saints" (KJV) or as "God's holy people" (NIV).

7) If the Holy Spirit is not the restrainer that is to be removed, then the *Left Behind* scenario that many Christians expect to transpire is fictitious. This concept has been a more recent development since the release of the book series and movie bearing the same name. According to this scenario, the sudden removal of Christians causes disruption worldwide. If Christians were flying planes, driving trains, and automobiles, performing surgery, or functioning in any other capacity, their sudden disappearance would cause chaos. However, this scheme only works if the Holy Spirit is the restrainer that is removed along with the church before Daniel's 70th week arrives. Otherwise, Christians would be undergoing severe persecution for not taking the mark of the beast. They would not be participating in the global economy because employment wouldn't be possible without the mark of the beast. They would not be flying planes, driving trains and automobiles, they would be hunted down and hiding.

This is why Dr. John MacArthur's teaching that a person can get the mark of the beast and still be redeemed is so deadly.[84] Under those circumstances people would readily compromise and take the mark of the beast. Imagine, what would happen when Daniel's 70th week does occur and the rapture hasn't happen yet. Those believing pretrib will be unprepared for being cut off economically, persecuted, jailed, and even put to death. Then there would be a modern-day Thessalonians situation where believers think they have entered the day of the Lord.

Jesus spoke of this circumstance when he declared, "Then you will be handed over to be persecuted and put to death, and you will be hated by all nations because of me. At that time many will turn away from the faith and will betray and hate each other (Matthew 24:9-10, NIV). "Jesus is saying that this will be especially the case in the last days. Perhaps the issues will be more clearly drawn then. Whether that is the reason or not, Jesus' followers are clearly warned that the end time will mean serious trouble for them."[85] Paul echoes this same warning when he writes about the "apostasy" (2 Thes. 2:3). This prophecy is concerning Christians abandoning the faith.

Secondly, Jesus stated, "If anyone wishes to come after Me, he must deny himself, and take up his cross and follow Me. "For whoever wishes to save his life will lose it; but whoever loses his life for My sake will find it. "For what will it profit a man if he gains the whole world and forfeits his soul? Or, what will a man give in exchange for his soul? "For the Son of Man is going to come in the glory of His Father with His angels, and will then repay every man according to his deeds" (Matthew 16:24-27). This is a powerful passage that has eschatological significance. Jesus states, if you lose your life for my sake, like those in Revelation 13:7, you will save it.

Revelation 14:9-12, declares you will suffer eternal destruction in the lake of fire for taking the mark of the beast. On one hand, Christians have been taught a pretrib rapture and promised that they wouldn't see the Antichrist. On the other hand, MacArthur, and others, teach you can take the mark of the beast and still be saved. Undoubtedly, beliefs like this will provide a rationale to take the mark of the beast, and cause Christians to compromise as many will during that time. The apostasy of which Paul spoke will be of such a magnitude, that it will be one of

---

84 https://www.youtube.com/watch?v=DTc8w5h8UTI accessed 4-17-20 Jimmy DeYoung and Brannon House, discussing and agreeing with MacArthur's mark of the beast position.
85 Pillar New Testament Commentary - The Gospel According to Matthew, pg 599

two signs that indicates the coming day of the Lord. So, what difference does it make if the restrainer is the Holy Spirit or not? I'm afraid it will make a big difference to a great number of Christians all over the world.

In the next editions of this *End-time Apologetics Series*, I will address other doctrinal issues with pre-trib rapture theory. This is just the beginning.

BIBLIOGRAPHY

Barnes, Albert *Barnes Notes on the Old Testament*, 1884-85 edition, Reprinted by Baker Books, 1996, Grand Rapids MI, *Daniel 10:21, The Book of Truth*

Bruce, F. F., *Word Biblical Commentary*, Volume 45, 1 & 2 Thessalonians, Thomas Nelson Publishers, 2002, pg 169

Adam Clarke, *Adam Clarke Commentary* , 1826, Baker Books, Grand Rapids MI., reprint 1970, *the restrainer*

Carson, Donald A., *NIV Zondervan Study Bible*, Zondervan, 2015, Grand Rapids, MI 2015, *The Book of Truth*, pg. 1712, Tremper Longman III *Who Is The Restrainer?* Jeffrey A.D. Weima, pg. 2453

Chadwick, Henry, *Encyclopedia Britannica Online*, Tertullian, attempted martyrdom of St. Apostle John, accessed 4/10/20 https://www.britannica.com/biography/Saint-John-the-Apostle

Cooper, Lamar Eugene, Sr. *The New American Commentary An Exegetical and Theological Exposition of Holy Scripture* Ezekiel, Volume 17, 1994 B & H Publishing Group, Nashville TN, pg 288, Daniel chap. 10

Danker, Frederick William, *A Greek-English Lexicon of the New Testament and Other Early Christian Literature*, (BDAG) 1957, 1979, 2000, University of Chicago Press, *apostasia, abyss, the comforter, legion, musterion*

Davids, Peter H. *Pillar New Testament Commentary* The Letters of 2 Peter and Jude, William B. Eerdmans Publishing, Grand Rapids, MI, Apollos Leichester England, 1991, Letter of St. Jude, *the glorious ones* pg 234

Deane, W.J. and W.S. Lewis, *The Pulpit Commentary*, Spence-Jones, H. D. M. (Henry Donald Maurice), 1836-1917, editor. The Pulpit Commentary. New York : London: Anson D.F. Randolph; Kegan Paul, Trench, 1883, *Zechariah, Angel of the Lord*

Delitzsch, Franz, and Carl Friedrich Keil. 1857. *Biblical commentary on the Old Testament*. Edinburgh: T. & T. Clark.Volume 9, pg 744, *Ezekiel, Daniel*

Dictionary of Christianity in America, Wipfand Stock Publishers, Eugene OR, by InterVarsity Press, 1990:
  R. McLaren, The Origin and Development of the Open Brethren in North America (1982); H. H. Rowdon, The Origins of the Brethren (1967). J. G. Stackhouse, *Plymouth Brethren*
  E. Sandeen, The Roots of Fundamentalism: British and American Millenarianism, 1800-1930 (1970); C. Bass, Backgrounds to Dispensationalism (1960); H. A. Ironside, An Historical Sketch of the Brethren Movement (1942). J. D. Hannah, *John Nelson Darby*
  C. B. Bass, Backgrounds to Dispensationalism (1960); C. N. Kraus, Dispensationalism in America (1958); C. C. Ryrie, Dispensationalism Today (1965); E. R. Sandeen, The Roots of Fundamentalism (1970). T. P. Weber, *Dispensationalism*
  G. M. Marsden, Fundamentalism and American Culture (1980); C. I. Scofield, Rightly Dividing the Word of Truth (1888). C. W. Whiteman, *Scofield Reference Bible*
  J. G. Melton, ed., Encyclopedia of American Religions (1986); J. O. Henry, For Such a Time as This, A History of the I.F.C.A. (1983). P. C. Wilt, *Bible Church Movement*
  J. D. Hannah, "The Social and Intellectual History of the Evangelical Theological College" (unpublished Ph.D. dissertation, University of Texas at Dallas, 1988). J. D. Hannah, *Lewis Sperry Chafer*

Geisler, Norman *Baker Encyclopedia of Christian Apologetics*, Baker Books Grand Rapids Michigan, 1999, *The Problem of Evil*, p. 222
  Geisler, Norman *Systematic Theology Vol. 4*, Bethany House, Minneapolis MN, 2005, pg 616, *Michael*

Holman Concise Topical Concordance, Holman Bible Publishers, 1998, Holman Concise Topical Concordance, *angels*

Kittel, Gerhard, *The Theological Dictionary of the New Testament*, Vol. 2, Eerdmans Publishing, Grand Rapids, MI, 1964, pg 829-30, *Katcheo*

MacArthur, John *The MacArthur New Testament Commentary*, 1 & 2 Thessalonians, Moody Publishers, Chicago, IL, 2001, *Michael vs. Satan* pg. 277, and 278, *removal of restrainer does not support pre-trib rapture.*
   MacArthur Bible Commentary, Thomas Nelson, Inc, 2005, Nashville TN, *Demon from the Abyss* pg 2028

Maza, Christine, *Newsweek* article *Trump Will Start the End of the World... https://www.newsweek.com/trump-will-bring-about-end-worldevangelicals-end-times-779643*, 1-12-2018, accessed 11-20-20.

Morris, Leon, *Pillar New Testament Commentary, The Gospel According to Matthew* by Wm. B. Eerdmans Publishing Co., 1992, Grand Rapids, MI

Pentecost, J. Dwight *Things To Come*, Zondervan, 1958 Grand Rapids, MI, chp. 17, pg 262, *The Restrainer*

Roberts, Alexander D.D. *Ante-Nicene Fathers Translations of The Writings of the Fathers Down to A. D. 325* The Rev. James Donaldson, LL.D., Volume 1, *The Martyrdom of Polycarp*

Spencer, Stephen R., *The Encyclopedia of Christianity* - Volume 1 (A-D), pg 885, *Dispensationalism*

Stanton, Gerald B., *Kept from the Hour*, Grand Rapids, Michigan: Zondervan Publishing House, 1956. Schoettle Publishing 1964, 1990, *Restrainer*

Strong, James, *The New Strong's Exhaustive Concordance of the Bible*, Thomas Nelson, 1990, Greek *zoon, therion, musterion, abyssos*, Hebrew Dictionary, *nus, chazaq*

Thomas, Robert L. *New American Standard, Hebrew Aramaic and Greek Dictionaries*, Foundation Publications, Inc., Anaheim, California 1981, 1998, *iddan*

Walvoord, John *The Bible Knowledge Commentary, New Testament* Published by David C. Cook 1983, Colorado Springs, CO, 2 Thes. 2, pg 717
   The Rapture Question, Zondervan, Grand Rapids, MI, 1957, pg 81

Weston, Emma Moore *The Story of Scofield's Life*, Condensed from J. M. Canfield's book *The Incredible Scofield*, Chalcedon/Ross House Books; 2nd edition (2005)

Zodhiates, Spiro *The Complete Word Study Dictionary, New Testament*, AMG Publishers, Chattanooga, TN, 1992, pg 61, *bottomless pit*

APPENDIX

The following information are the actual letters and paper in the exchange between the author and Drs. Walvoord and Pentecost. The handwritten notations on the paper are those of J. Dwight Pentecost. In order to understand the context of Dr. Pentecost's notations and the letters from Pentecost and Walvoord, you must to read the whole paper. By doing so, all of the comments will be kept in context and give greater insight to my rebuttals throughout the book. The redacted items contain personal information.

5-9-97

Dr E. Dwight Pentecost
Dallas Theological Seminary
3909 Swiss Ave.
Dallas Tx. 75204

Dear Dr. Pentecost:

I am Min. Dennis J. Woods, author of *"Unlocking the Door: A Key to Biblical Prophecy,"* published by Huntington House Publishers © 1994. The reason why I am writing to you is so that you may review a paper that I've written titled, **The Holy Angels, God's Ministers of Restraint.** The topic of angelic restraint is one of the focuses of my book.

Dr. Pentecost I humbly request that you render an objective opinion of the position which I espouse. Please, by all means be critical. Since I use your text as a bases for some of my arguments, I feel it is appropriate that you respond to my arguments. By no means am I critical of you as a renown theologian with a world wide reputation. But my main concern is with the church at large, and what could happen if in fact current dispensational theories were incorrect.

You should know that I did send Dr. Walvoord a reversion of this paper back in the summer of 1996 while I was living in the Dallas area. Though Dr. Walvoord disagreed with my position, he didn't really say why, nor did he refute what I had said. Therefore, that could *almost* be interpreted as acquiescing. To avoid this, I have included some questions at the end of the paper to be answered, and I also invite your commentary.

Dr. Pentecost I know you're a busy man. And I am not a renowned theologian like you are. I also realize that don't carry enough academic status for you to take time to respond to. But as a follow minister of the gospel, I humbly ask you to please do so. I believe in sound doctrine, and if I'm in error, then show me, that I may accurately glorify our Lord and Savior Jesus Christ to the best of my ability.

Please return all correspondence t

May the grace and peace of Lord and Savior Jesus Christ continue with you always. In Jesus name.

Sincerely,

Min. Dennis J. Woods

The Holy Angels
God's Ministers of Restraint
Rev. 20:1-3
By: Dennis J. Woods

If one could disqualify, disprove or discredit a major tenet of any theory, it may very well diminish or destroy that theory's validity. If when formulating any given hypothesis, you fail to figure in all obvious, relevant and available factors, the suppositions and conclusions derived from such an incomplete investigation, can prove faulty and will inevitably lead to flawed conclusions. Consequently, the integrity of such a theory is compromised and it's foundation could collapse under the weight of critical analysis and scrutiny.

In view of the stated proposition, major tenets of the Pre-tribulation Rapture Theory, could possibly fall into the category of flawed. This theory is supported by faulty presuppositions and conclusions which can be attributed to a failure to factor in all obvious, relevant and available biblical facts. One of the most critically flawed presuppositions in pretribulationism is the necessary and emphatic reliance on the "He" and the "What," of Second Thessalonians chapter two, being that of the Holy Spirit Himself.

The necessity of this interpretation is under scored in Dr. James Walvoord's, The Rapture Question. In this book Dr. Walvoord asserts: While other passages of scripture and tenets of the pre- trib rapture theory are in the realm of the debatable. If left unsupported by other scriptural text, interpreting the "He" of 2 Thessalonians 2:7, as the Holy Spirit restraining force, by itself seems to constitute a confirmation of a pre-tribulation rapture. (Text was not available when writing paper, quoted from memory).

It should be noted that the pre-trib theory uses several scriptural passages to support that

but not the basis of pre trib

view based method on literal interpretation

view however, according to Dr. Walvoord and others, 2 Thessalonians seems to be one of the most definitive passages to support the theory. In other expositions such as found in the Scofield Reference Bible's commentary, employs exclusive language such as, "This person can be **NO OTHER THAN** the Holy Spirit in the Church." (Emphasis mine)

The logical conclusion then reach is: the Holy Spirit-the restrainer (the He) who is resident in the church, is to be *taken out of the way*. Therefore, the Church, who is the corporate temple of the Holy Spirit, will also have to be removed at such time, when the Holy Spirit is removed from earth. Thus fore the rapture will have to occur when the Holy Spirit is removed. This is all to occur prior to the revealing of the anti-Christ. The conclusion is, the rapture will occur prior to the tribulation period, coinciding with the out taking of the Holy Spirit.

The validity of this theory, heavily but not exclusively, depends on interpreting the Holy Spirit as the only **CAPABLE** agent of restraint, which according to 2 Thessalonians 2, is to be taken out of the way. Therefore, in support of the Pre-trib theory it becomes the necessary interpretation which is espoused emphatically by numerous scholars who hold this view. And it also serves as the flagship passage that supports this theory.

In order for me to expose the flawed premise of the Holy Spirit only, aspect of this theory. I must refer to another well known and probably the most comprehensive text available on pretribulationism, which is, "Things to Come," by Dr. E. Dwight Pentecost. In his book, Dr. Pentecost mounts a seemingly insurmountable case for the Holy Sprit only, restraining force of 2 Thessalonians chapter two. Before he states his case he first refutes the historic attempts to identify the restraining force, and he does a good job. To reenforce the pre-trib view, Dr. Pentecost quotes from Gerald Stanton's, "Kept From the Hour," when making his case. The following is a brief of the arguments that Dr. Pentecost uses to defend the restraining ministry of

the Holy Spirit, which is found on page 262, of Things to Come. Dr. Pentecost asserts:

(1). By mere elimination, the Holy Spirit MUST be the restrainer. All other suggestions fall far short of meeting the requirements.

(2). The wicked one is a personality, and his operations include the realm of the spiritual. The restrainer must like wise be a personality and a spiritual being to hold anti-Christ in check until the time of his revealing. Mere agencies or impersonal spiritual forces would be inadequate.

(3). The restrainer MUST be a member of the Godhead, and stronger than the man of sin and satan who energizes him. In order to restrain evil down through the course of the age, the restrainer MUST be eternal. The theater of sin is the entire world therefore, it is imperative that the restrainer be one who is not limited by time or space.

Now if left uncontested, the Holy Spirit only interpretation seems to be the only valid

possibility. But what if there is another biblical possibility that's obvious, relevant, and available,

yet overlooked? Considering that, would the Holy Spirit restrainer, interpretation remain the

absolute and only qualifying interpretation? If there has been an overlooked possibility, How

badly would the pre-trib theory, as we know it, be undermined? The fact is if there is another *not at all since pre trib is not based only on this passage*

viable biblical interpretation, then a chain reaction of questions and doubts begin to move

throughout other significant tenets of the theory.

Since the Apostle Paul does not tell us who the restrainer is, no matter whether one does

an exeges in the original languages or not, the information is simply not there. Therefore we must

fill in the blanks. At this point the pre-trib theorist must resort to using theological conjecture,

coupled with other passages of scripture, that are at best implicit, and highly theoretical. All this *?.*

is fine if there is no other possible restraining force to be identified. But what if there is something

or someone else? One might ask how could it be missed for so long? At that question I am most

baffled.

false

In exposing the (Achilles heel) of pretribulationism lets examine Revelation 20:1-3. The text reads:

refers to Christ frequently in Revelation - 10:1-11

  And I saw an (angel) come down from heaven, having the key to the bottomless pit and a great chain in his hand. (vs.2) And he laid hold on the dragon, that old serpent, which is the Devil and Satan, and bound him a thousand years, (vs. 3) And cast him into the   bottomless pit, and shut him up, and set a seal upon him, that he should deceive the nations no more, till the thousand years should be fulfilled: and after that he must be loosed a little season. (KJV)

Here we have a single unnamed angelic being, who is the lone agent of restraint, who binds and imprisons satan himself, the chief evil principality and power in the entire universe. This angel possessed the key to the bottomless pit (the abyss) and locked satan in for a period of one thousand years. *2 Thess 2 refers to restraint on Satanic activity during this age — Rev 20*

  Now lets go back to the fundamental tenets sighted by Dr. Pentecost, where he builds his case for the Holy Spirit ONLY argument. With the above stated text, and others, I will methodically dismantle Dr. Pentecost's most decisive arguments. Again, using "Things to Come," page 262, Dr. Pentecost quoting from Gerald Stanton's, "Kept From the Hour," asserts:

(1). *Pentecost/Stanton:* By mere elimination, the Holy Spirit <u>MUST BE</u> the restrainer. All other suggestions fall far short of meeting the requirements.

A). *Woods* **The argument begins with the statement: *by mere elimination.* However, angels were never included among the ranks of the eliminated. By angels not being considered, the argument starts out on a faulty basis. Clearly all biblical possibilities were not examined nor covered, thus a false pretense that all qualifying possibilities were eliminated.** *where?*

B). **Rev. 20:1-3, and other passages in both old and new testaments show angels are more than capable, and do in fact restrain. In the case of Rev. 20, the devil himself is the one who** is restrained.

C). In order to maintain a credible theory one must factor in all the relevant and available variables, or you simply haven't covered all of the bases. Though Pentecost and Stanton argue effectively against historical attempts to identify the restrainer, they missed and obvious one, ANGELS !

(2). *Pentecost/Stanton:* The wicked one is a personality, and his operations include the realm of the spiritual. The restrainer must like wise be a personality, and a spiritual being to hold anti-Christ in check until the time of his revealing.

A). *Woods:* Angels are indeed spiritual beings, hence personalities, who operate in both physical and spiritual realms.

B). Though angels are normally unnamed, they are referred to in the masculine gender.

C). If angels can restrain satan, then restraining a satanic subordinate (i.e. anti-Christ) would be no problem.

(3). *Pentecost/Stanton:* The restrainer MUST BE a member of the Godhead. STRONGER then the anti-christ and satan who energizes him. In order to restrain evil down through the course of the age, the restrainer MUST BE eternal, and not limited by time or space.

A). *Woods:* Each one of these arguments is unequivicably wrong!! Holy angels, restrain demonic principalities (Dan. 10) and even satan himself who is the ultimate expression of evil in existence. Although this angel is holy, he is NOT a member of the GODHEAD.

B). In Rev. 12, Michael and his angels fought against the devil and his angels and the text explicitly states that the devil was not STRONG ENOUGH for Michael and his angelic army. (NIV)

C). Clearly angels are indeed strong enough to restrain satan and obviously any satanic subordinates. However, though angels are immortal they are NOT ETERNAL. They like satan are created finite beings. In addition to this, the premise that the restrainer needs to be eternal to restrain evil down through the course of the age is also faulty. The forces that oppose satan's heavenly rebellion only needed to present since the time of that rebellion, not all eternity. Prior to the rebellion, there was no manifestation of evil to restrain. Before the point of the rebellion and on, holy angels were present, but since they are spiritual beings, and immortal, they aren't hindered by time nor space. Holy angels are also numerous enough to check each demon, and out number them by a two to one ratio. This is at least implied in rev. chap. 12:4, and explicit in Dan. 10:13. Theoretically, no matter where in the universe angelic evil exist, there is enough godly angels to check them, in that sense not even omnipresence is absolutely necessary. *angels never act independently - They are always under Gods authority*

Now by no means am I suggesting that the Holy Spirit, can't or never, restrains evil. The Holy Spirit is God and nothing is impossible with him. However it's interesting that we would assume that nothing less than God could restrain evil in the first place. Just as man is ontologically lower than angels, so are angels lower than God. No matter what rank an angel holds, he's simply no match for the Almighty. No angelic being has ever been, nor will ever be, a threat to God's sovereignty. By implication we seem to mistakenly treat satan as God's opposite equal. God doesn't have to dirty his hands by personally restraining the devil. But, he has delegated that to ranks of the holy angelic host. *So they act under His authority. Even if angels are agents*

Now that I've proven that there has been an unrestrained oversight in pre-trib theory, the question remains, What's all this have to do with the revealing of the anti-Christ? To answer this *it is still God who restrains* question lets look at another passage of scripture found in Rev. 17:8, the passage reads:

The beast that thou sawest was, and is not; and shall ascend out of the bottomless pit, and go into perdition: and they that dwell on the earth shall wonder, whose names are not written in the book of life from the foundation of the world, when they behold the beast that was, and is not, and yet is. (KJV)

Now this is a very interesting passage which has some very important information in it. Though it is significant, many expositors have either overlooked it and or explained away its relevance. Although there are probably many ways to interpret this passage, I will be examining two interpretations espoused by prominent pretribulationist.

The first is: (A) this passage is concerning the emergence of the reconstructed Roman empire under satanic influence. Or: (B) this passage is in reference to satan himself, emerging up from the abyss. Lets begin with the first interpretation; the reconstructed Roman Empire. In examining *A*, there is a political, historical, and futuristic aspect of the 7 heads 10 horns metaphor. But to interpret this passage as the reconstructed Roman Empire alone, doesn't do justice to the text. Why? Because, since it is the Abyss from where this monstrosity is ascending, we must ask the question, What do the scriptures tell us about the abyss? And what do the scriptures tell us about what's in the abyss? In either case I don't think governments, agencies and kingdoms come from the abyss. However we will see that demonic principalities and powers do.

As Rev. 20:7 tells the abyss is indeed a prison, where even the devil himself can and will be detained, rendering him quite powerless. The scriptures imply that this place is escape proof, under angelic guard and supervision, and under lock and key Now whether the passage is just speaking metaphorically or not, the point is, the abyss is a secured place of detention.

Though I do understand that you can't set tight doctrinal boundaries around the symbols and metaphors found in apocalyptic literature. Undoubtedly, someone will argue that this passage is too metaphorical to interpret definitively. Well to that I would agree with to a certain extent. So with that in mind, lets turn to the gospel narratives to see if we can find some continuity in relationship to demons and the abyss.

In three gospel accounts, Matthew, Mark and Luke, we find the story of the maniac of Gadara. In Matthew 8:29 coupled with Luke 8:31, we can easily deduce that the demons which possessed this man begged Jesus not to command to go into the abyss before their appointed time. Also in the book of Jude vs. 6, there is also a reference to the angels who left their first estate, who are reserved under restraint in everlasting chains. And finally, if you take into account Rev. 11:7, this passage tells us that the two witnesses are finally overcome by the beast, at the end of their 3 and half year prophetic ministry. However, the credit doesn't go to the human counterpart of the beast, it goes to the beast that ascended out of the bottomless pit. By this time the beast is released from the bottomless pit, or else he wouldn't be able to overcome the two witnesses. When you consider all these passages, I don't think you have done the rev. 17:8 passage justice to simply say, the reconstructed Roman empire is all that's in focus here. I believe the passage clearly portrays a demonic personality also referred to as the beast.

The second interpretation is, this is Satan himself. Although this is getting warm, it too misses the mark. In the book of the Revelation, the devil, serpent, and dragon are all synonyms for satan. Devil is used 5 times, serpent is used 4 times, and dragon is used 12 times (speaking directly of satan) and one other time speaking indirectly of him. These descriptive nouns are used singularly or in combination with one another. When the book of the revelation wants to highlight satan, these descriptive nouns are also used in conjunction with the 7 head 10 horn imagery. For example, in Rev. 12, the 7 head, 10 horn imagery, is clearly referring to satan. In this passage all of the descriptive nouns are used. However in Rev. 13, the 7 head, 10 horn imagery, is referring to the anti-christ. However, to illustrate where the beast is getting his power from, the descriptive noun dragon is used to identify satan, who is the second power player of the passage. So we can see every time the 7 heads, 10 horn imagery is used, we need to be clear on who it's referring to, whether it's the anti-christ or satan.

In the case of Rev. 17, none of the descriptive nouns that identify satan are used in the entire chapter. In verses 7 through 16, clearly show the 7 heads 10 horn imagery from the aspect of the beast. If you interpret this passage to mean satan, then some more relevant information is over looked. What's overlooked, is the demonic aspect of the beast, to which the 7 heads, 10 horn imagery applies, who is resident in the abyss. This is extremely relevant when considering what's holding back the revealing (apokalupto) of the anti-christ.

As Daniel 9:27 states, the individual who will become the beast, (technically he's in that role for only 42 months) begins the 70th week as some sort of statesman who is an advocate of peace. He inaugurates a peace covenant with many for seven years, and also allows Israel to go back to their daily sacrifice and oblations. Then right in the middle of this period, he becomes the evil tyrant of Rev. 13, seen rising up from the sea of humanity, bearing the imagery of the 7 heads, 10 horns.

In Rev. 17:7-8, the angel begins to tell John, the hidden truth (mystery) about the beast, particularly that the beast shall ascend out of the bottomless pit. It is therefore obvious that the two, Rev.13 human dictator, and the Rev. 17, demonic principality, aspects of the beast are closely related. Though satan does give anti-christ his power, seat and great authority. It is also conceivable that the beast out of the bottomless pit is the principality who actually possess the anti-christ. This is why he goes from his peace persona, the first half of the 70th week, to the beast, who has the 7 heads, 10 horns imagery, the last half of the 70th week. According to the angelic interpretation (Rev. 17:7-8) these symbols (7 heads 10 horns) are actually attributed to the beast, out of the bottomless pit.

With this in mind, the question is, How does the beast that's in the bottomless pit, get out of this secured place of detention? Remember, not even satan can get out of there. Now if satan can be locked in the abyss for a predetermined amount of time, rendered powerless, without the possibility of escape, then why shouldn't that apply to any other being held in the abyss? If satan himself was restrained by one unnamed holy angel who has the responsibility to lock and unlock, and cast the devil into the abyss. Then why wouldn't that apply to other beings in the abyss as well? (cf Jude vs. 6).

As long as the beast is in the bottomless pit, it's absolutely impossible for him to become active in the earth realm, as it relates to his role in revelation 13. (I'm not speaking of the spirit of anti-christ already at work, as John refers to in his epistles). While in the pit, the demonic aspect of the beast is absolutely prevented from manifesting himself in the human dictator. Since the abyss is a place, the use of, "what" that withholds (2 Thes. 2:6) is appropriate. Since angels, who are referred to in the masculine gender, are clearly portrayed as God's agents of restraint. The "HE" of 2 Thes. 2:7, is also appropriate.   *but God is the restrainer*

Please understand that I'm not claiming that the Greek grammar in 2 Thessalonians 2, paints the same picture that I've painted here. But what I'm saying is, Since Paul didn't say what the "WHAT" is, or who the "HE" was, we can either opt for, implicit text and theological assumptions or deal with some explicit text that deal directly with the anti-christ, as to: where he's bound, where he must ascend from, the agents of restrain, the responsibility for binding and incarcerating demons in the abyss. Hey I didn't write this. The apostle John did. The question is why aren't we using the information in, our theories?

Now after you factor in all of what I've said thus far, I will pose the question: Is the holy Sprit restrainer, the only biblical option? The answer is an emphatic no! Well if the He and What of second Thessalonians is not the holy Spirit, then what effect will that have on the viability of the pre-trib theory? Since the traditional interpretation of the He and What, Holy Spirit restrainer interpretation, is so critical to the theory, it starts an avalanche of uncertainty. If pre-trib theory is right, and we're out of here before the seventieth week, than hallelujah. But what if it's wrong? What are the ramifications, particularly in a country where persecution for the faith isn't life threatening, like it was for Christians in the days of the Thessalonians. Would modern day Christians remain faithful under severe persecution as have past generations of church saints? What would be the impact be on Christians who expected to be raptured away prior to the 70th week, that now find themselves in the midst of what they have been taught was the beginning of the wrath of God, be. Could there be a generation of modern day Thessalonians, whose faith was shaken, because they thought the Day of the Lord had already begun.

What if it wasn't the Holy Spirit, that Paul was referring to in 2 Thessalonians 2, then the necessity for the Holy Spirit in the church, and the church, to be removed prior to the revealing wouldn't be absolutely necessary. How comforting would an eschatological theory be at that point? What if God intended for the church to use, all the information in the book of the revelation, not explain away its relevance. What if God, wanted Christians to know, no matter how bad things get, anti-christ or not, those who names are written in the lambs book of life will not bow down to the anti-christ. Did other generations of believer have the luxury of opting out of facing other anti-christ's, with the attitude that God won't let that happen to us? Is God obligated to honor our theories?

Would we today have the faith of Polycarp, who was a church age, holy spirit filled believer, just as we are? Is our generation of saints beyond facing our time of trouble? If the Church began with severe persecution, who we to think it can't close that way. What if part of the reason some will fall away is because, people were told they were not going to be here when the trouble starts, yet find themselves in the middle of it. It already happened once at Thessalonica, could history repeat itself?

It should be noted that what I've developed here *is not* a **COMPLETE** argument. I intentionally only focused in on certain aspects of my argument to open up a dialog and pose some questions. I clearly understand that Pre-trib theory *is not* **SOLELY** based on just second Thessalonians. My Holy Spirit restrainer argument, only opens the can of worms, and trust me, without that pre-trib 2 Thessalonians 2, interpretation, there's a lot of other worms to be reckoned with.

In my closing, I'm NOT attempting to eisege, the ideas of my paper into the 2 Thes. 2 text. I'm simply saying, in the absence of identifying information in 2 Thes. 2, Why wouldn't we use relevant, explicit eschatological passages that directly answer these questions in a biblically pragmatic way?

but you imply by discounting the Holy Spirit view you have destroyed pre-trib

CRITICAL QUESTIONS

Note: Please answer these questions, considering all that I have put forth in this paper:

1). Why have theorist opted for implicit scriptures to identify the He who now letteth, when there are explicit eschatological passage that deal directly with his idenity? And why have these passage been overlooked?

2). Why can't angels be the restrainers? *They can be agents but only under authority. You make them independent*

3). Since the scriptures tell us that the beast ascends out of the bottomless pit, Why can't the abyss be what's holding the beast back/down? (think about it, if he's in the bottomless pit, how can he be uncovered, unless he's let out)

but who put him there?

is This Satan or antichrist.

DALLAS THEOLOGICAL SEMINARY

May 20, 1997

Mr. Dennis J. Woods
P.O. Box 1213
Harvey, IL   60426

Dear Mr. Woods:

As you asked, I have gone over the material you sent to me, and have made a few comments on it. As you would expect I find myself out of agreement with your position.

You seem to feel that in establishing angels as the restrainers you have destroyed pretribulationism. This is a fallacy. You have attacked only one of the bases for the position. You must be familiar with Walvoord's 49 reasons for the pretrib. view since you refer to his work.

To assume as you do that the pretrib view rests on 2 Thess. 2 iswrong. Many pretrib supporters use that passage only to support the view they base on other passages, not to prove it.

A serious weakness in your view attributes sovereignty to angels, wereas in Scripture they always act under divine authority. Even though they may may be agents in restraintit is still God (the Holy Spirit) who actually restrains.

I consider that I have said all I intend to say on your view and do not expect to carry on further discussion about it.

Sincerely yours

J. Dwight Pentecost

J. Dwight Pentecost

DALLAS THEOLOGICAL SEMINARY

June 19, 1996

Mr. Dennis James Woods
3211 Irving Blvd.
Dallas, TX 75247

Dear Mr. Woods:

Your manuscript on "The Holy Angels: God's Ministers of Restraint" has been examined. I frankly do not follow your reasoning or your material. You do not seem to realize that this is only a small portion of the pretribulational position, and you do not answer the many other indications that the rapture is before the tribulation.

Obviously you have not examined correctly what it means for the Holy Spirit to be removed as stated in 2 Thessalonians 2. It may be true that the exegesis is not entirely clear, but in some cases we need to move to the major passages such as 1 Thessalonians 4 and 5, and the earlier portion of 2 Thessalonians 2 that clearly places the rapture before the revelation of the man of sin and he is going to be revealed more than seven years before the Second Coming according to other Scriptures, such as Daniel 9:27.

No doubt none of us are entirely correct in all of our understanding but I cannot follow your arguments nor your conclusions.

I am returning your manuscript.

Sincerely yours in Christ,

John F. Walvoord
Chancellor

JFW:fgt

3909 SWISS AVENUE • DALLAS, TEXAS 75204 • (214) 824-3094

ABOUT THE AUTHOR

Dr. Dennis J. Woods has studied eschatology for over 40 years. His fascination with biblical prophecy began in 1976 after reading his first Hal Lindsey book while serving in the Navy onboard the U.S.S. England. In 1982, after being honorably discharged, he continued his eschatological studies reading great dispensational authors.

In 1994, Dr. Woods' first book Unlocking the Door: A Key to Biblical Prophecy was published, giving him national exposure. In 1995, he further sharpened his eschatological skills by taking a Revelation course taught by renowned New Testament theologian Dr. D.A. Carson, at Trinity Evangelical Divinity School, Wisconsin extension, Elm Brook Church. In 1996, he also corresponded with Dallas Theological Seminary pillars Dr. John Walvoord (2004) and in 1997 with J. Dwight Pentecost (2014).

Today, Dr. Woods is President and CEO of Life To Legacy, LLC, a thriving independent book publisher has published over 50 titles. He is also the pastor of Power of the Holy Ghost Deliverance Ministries, having nursing home and radio outreach ministries in Chicago IL. Dr. Woods also host the Revelation Revolution PODCAST. In 2004, Dr. Woods received his Doctorate of Biblical Studies from Midwest Theological Institute of Indiana.

All speaking engagement requests for the author should be submitted to: Life2legacybooks@att.net

About the Publisher

Let us bring your story to life! With Life to Legacy, we offer the following publishing services: manuscript development, editing, transcription services, ghostwriting, cover design, copyright services, ISBN assignment, worldwide distribution, and eBooks.

Throughout the entire production process, you maintain control over your project. Even if you have no manuscript, we can ghost-write your story for you from audio recordings or legible handwritten documents. Whether print-on-demand or trade publishing, we have publishing packages to meet your needs. We make the production and publishing processes easy for you.

We also specialize in family history books, so you can leave a written legacy for your children, grandchildren, and others. You put your story in our hands, and we'll bring it to literary life!

Please visit our Web site:
www.Life2Legacy.com or call us at:
877-267-7477
You can also e-mail us at: Life2Legacybooks@att.net